Economic Integration
in the Western Hemisphere

EDITED BY

ROBERTO BOUZAS
AND
JAIME ROS

University of Notre Dame Press

Notre Dame   London

Library of Congress Cataloging-in-Publication Data

Economic integration in the western hemisphere / Roberto Bouzas and
Jaime Ros, editors.
    p.   cm.
    Includes bibliographical references.
    ISBN 0-268-00930-9
    1. Latin America—Economic integration—Case studies.   I. Bouzas,
Roberto.   II. Ros, Jaime.
HC125.E3737   1994
    337.1′8—dc20   94-15937
                                                            CIP

ECONOMIC INTEGRATION
IN THE WESTERN HEMISPHERE

A Title from the Helen Kellogg Institute
for International Studies

CONTENTS

FOREWORD

Despite the publicity that has attended the initiation of NAFTA and the plethora of other multilateral and bilateral trading agreements in Latin America in the early 1990s, efforts to promote regional trade in the Western Hemisphere are not without precedent. For more than a generation, regional trading agreements among the nations of the region have been proposed and attempted as strategies to overcome traditional regional obstacles to development. In an area where development was historically tied to economic links with nations outside the region, trade for a long time meant relations *hacia afuera,* outside the region, rather than *hacia adentro,* among the nations of the region themselves. Although the stereotypical patterns of trade in goods and services with Europe and the United States brought periods of prosperity to Latin America, especially in the last century, they also grounded explanations, like those in the dependency literature, for the failures of Latin American countries to achieve self-sustaining economic development.

However, the protectionist regimes that were introduced as an antidote, especially after World War II, soon revealed their own limitations, including those imposed by national restrictions of trade to domestic markets that were inadequate to sustain emerging industries. So, a generation ago there were various attempts to graft schemes for regional economic integration onto an assortment of separate and inward-looking domestic economic regimes. Some, like the Latin American Free Trade Area, attempted to be inclusive in membership by restricting the scope of regional integration to limited trade in goods and services. Others, like the Central American Common Market, had more limited membership, but a more comprehensive scope for the proposed regional economic integration.

For the most part, the uneasy unions of relatively autarkic domestic economic regimes with schemes for regional economic integration failed to flourish for long. Now, however, the vast majority of Latin American nations have embraced, along with democratic political regimes, domestic economic models that favor strong reliance on free markets that are open to the international movement of goods, services, and the factors of production. And so new possibilities have emerged for regional economic integration, sometimes under the old names, sometimes even including the colossus of the north, whose economic influence in the hemisphere earlier versions of Latin American integration sought to neutralize or avoid.

Realizing that the implications of regional schemes of economic integration for the newly open and market-driven Latin American economies are likely to be more significant than the effects of earlier attempts at regional integration, the Kellogg Institute chose the theme of hemispheric economic integration as the first in its annual series of programs on major issues affecting Latin America at the turn of the century, known as Project Latin America 2000 and supported by The Coca-Cola Company. The present volume is an outgrowth of the first series, which included an academic workshop and a public policy forum on the subject, bringing together scholars as well as business leaders, policymakers, labor leaders, and other practitioners from private and public sectors. Individual chapters in the present volume are devoted to each of the major current systems of regional economic integration and authored by scholars with special competence in the respective systems, along with overviews and comparative analysis by the distinguished co-editors, who also organized the academic workshop and participated in the public policy forum on Latin American economic integration at the Kellogg Institute. We are indebted to the editors and authors for enabling us to assemble so comprehensive an analysis and evaluation of the new diversity of possibilities and challenges facing the development of Latin America and the Western Hemisphere that is exemplified in the emerging initiatives for regional economic integration.

Ernest Bartell, C.S.C.
Executive Director
Helen Kellogg Institute for International Studies

THE NORTH-SOUTH VARIETY OF ECONOMIC INTEGRATION
Issues and Prospects for Latin America

Roberto Bouzas and Jaime Ros

Not more than a decade ago, economic integration and trade discrimination were in full discredit both in the United States and in Latin America.[1] In Latin America, the collapse of intraregional trade flows and the establishment of (almost) unprecedented trade barriers following the debt crisis gave the final blow to the regional integration attempts of the 1960s and 1970s. In the United States, the characteristic postwar emphasis upon multilateralism and unconditional most-favored-nation (MFN) principles still continued to effectively influence the practice of trade policy.

In this context, the idea of comprehensive and reciprocal liberalization arrangements between the United States and selected Latin American partners seemed remote, if not completely off the mark. More generally, the notion of a hemispheric free-trade agreement (FTA) would have been regarded as too eccentric even to merit consideration.

Yet a few years later, not only has the North American Free Trade Agreement (NAFTA) been successfully negotiated by Canada, Mexico, and the United States, but a rebirth of economic integration initiatives has swept the Western Hemisphere. Long-standing arrangements have been reinvigorated and fresh bilateral and minilateral deals have flourished all over the region. Furthermore, the pros and cons of FTA arrangements between the United States and the Latin American countries have also turned into an issue of debate as NAFTA negotiations have anticipated the emergence of a North-South variety of economic integration. To the

1

surprise of many, trade discrimination and economic integration have become seasoned again.

This sea-change in perceptions and practice has been the result of an interplay of global and domestic trends that have deeply affected the objectives and content of trade policy in both parts of the Western Hemisphere. On one side, the binding financial constraint brought about by the debt crisis and the increased awareness as to the policy implications of far-reaching internationalization of the world economy created a dysfunction between Latin America's new perceived imperatives and its old trade regime, providing a new rationale for economic integration in a context of trade liberalization. On the other side, the relative decline of the economic and technological leadership of the United States and the growing conviction that multilateral arrangements are today less effective than in the past for fostering U.S. trade and policy objectives contributed to the analogous perception that U.S. economic interests may now be best served by complementing the traditional approach with a strengthened bilateral and minilateral drive.

Do these new conditions create a common interest in the two sides of the Western Hemisphere as far as trade and investment links are concerned? If so, is this common interest best served by pulling together markets and resources? What challenges are the Latin American countries likely to face if the process is to go ahead? These questions underline some crucial policy issues that require answers if the risks and opportunities of reciprocal trade discrimination in the Western Hemisphere are to be adequately grasped.

The rebirth of discriminatory trade arrangements in the Western Hemisphere raises many important issues. This paper focuses upon the implications for the Latin American countries of one of its major new features: the emergence of a North-South variety of economic integration as inaugurated by NAFTA. The first section reviews some attributes of "new vintage" discriminatory arrangements in the Western Hemisphere. The second section offers a survey of existing theoretical arguments and empirical evidence regarding the allocative and dynamic gains stemming from the North-South variety of economic integration. The third section explores the factors influencing the structure of "positive" incentives for the Latin American countries to enter into North-

South discriminatory arrangements. The fourth section addresses some political economy issues that illustrate the path-dependence nature of the North-South variety of economic integration. Finally, a concluding section highlights the major points that can be drawn from the previous discussion.

I. Preferential Liberalization in the Western Hemisphere: Old and New

The revival of preferential liberalization policies in the Western Hemisphere in the late 1980s could be regarded as a reiteration of an old theme. After all, the quest for economic integration has been a lasting feature of Latin American relations for most of the postwar period. Similarly, and notwithstanding its multilateralist pledge, discrimination has been all but absent from U.S. trade policies ever since World War II. Yet, the nature and incentives of U.S. and Latin American discriminatory trade policies have changed considerably in recent years.

"Old Vintage" Discrimination

Despite the clear-cut predominance of multilateralism, discrimination has been a persistent feature of U.S. trade policies in the postwar period. Prominent examples include the exclusion of communist countries from the application of the MFN principle, the negotiation of the U.S.-Canada Auto Pact, the enactment of the Generalized System of Preferences (GSP) and, more recently, the implementation of the Caribbean Basin Initiative (CBI) and the U.S.-Israel Free Trade Agreement.[2] Trade discrimination has also been typical of the Latin American landscape, as illustrated by the establishment of ambitious regional and subregional integration schemes in the 1960s and 1970s and the long-lasting pledge to obtain preferential market access to developed country markets.

In the postwar period, preferential liberalization served different purposes in the United States and Latin America and, overall, played a subordinate role in the design of their trade policies and economic strategies. In the United States, discrimination ranked second to nonpreferential trade liberalization (tariff cuts) under the auspices of the General Agreement on Trade and Tariffs (GATT), and it involved a relatively minor portion of total

U.S. foreign trade. In practice, preferences became instrumental in punishing and rewarding selected partners, usually on security and/or foreign-policy grounds. The economic and technological leadership of the United States, its initially strong trade stance and mounting East-West confrontation provided the background and rationale for the use of trade discrimination as a foreign policy tool. (For a review of the determinants of U.S. trade policy in the 1950s and 1960s, see Baldwin, 1988.)

In Latin America, trade discrimination also was a subordinate policy, but with the objective of fostering domestic industrialization. By extending markets and eventually allowing the benefits of economies of scale and specialization to be reaped, regional integration was supposed to compensate for the compound inefficiencies of smallness and high protection.[3] The combined influence of low initial levels of intraregional trade, disputes as to the distribution of costs and benefits, and powerful domestic coalitions opposed to (even intraregional) trade liberalization contributed to the dismal record of regional and subregional economic integration schemes. (For a useful review of this experience in the 1960s and 1970s, see Tussie, 1987, and Mace, 1988.) As a complement, the Latin American countries also favored discrimination in their trade relations vis-à-vis the industrialized North. Since reciprocity and unconditional MFN treatment were regarded as inadequate in view of the large disparities in economic development and industrialization levels prevailing between developed and developing countries, the demand for preferential market access became recurrent.

The juxtaposition of the Latin American pledge for preferential treatment and the emphasis of the United States on multilateralism occurred whenever the latter was persuaded that diplomatic and/or security considerations were at stake. This explains to a large extent the adoption of the Generalized System of Preferences in 1974 (vigorously pressed by developing countries at the United Nations Conference on Trade and Development) as well as the implementation of the Caribbean Basin Initiative in 1983. It is also helpful in placing into broader context other U.S.-sponsored (or tolerated) preferential arrangements, such as the European Payments Union (EPU) (and later the European Coal and Steel Community [ECSC] and the European Economic Community

[EEC]), the U.S.-Israel Free Trade Agreement, and even the U.S.-Canada Auto Pact.

"New Vintage" Discrimination?

During the late 1980s, preferential liberalization gained new impetus in the Western Hemisphere (see Appendix 1). Previous arrangements such as the Central American Common Market (CACM), the Andean Group, and the Caribbean Community (Caricom) have been given new life and new foci. Other fresh bilateral and minilateral arrangements have also flourished as illustrated, among others, by the U.S.-Canadian Free Trade Agreement (CUSFTA), the North American Free Trade Agreement (NAFTA), the Southern Common Market (Mercosur), and the Chile-Mexico FTA.

This "new vintage" of preferential trade arrangements in the Western Hemisphere displays a number of distinctive features as compared to the past. On the one hand, it links for the first time (either in talk or actual negotiations) countries from the North and South along the lines of reciprocal arrangements. On the other, new arrangements are taking place against a background of far-reaching trade liberalization in the South. Largely as a result of United States interest, "new" and "brand-new" issues have been included into the negotiating agenda, extending the latter well beyond the realm of tariff rates and trade in goods.

These new features fit the changing domestic and international conditions in which trade policies are being designed and implemented, in both the United States and Latin America. Three influences must be singled out in the case of the United States: i) the relative decline of its economic and technological might (as made apparent by mounting trade deficits, loss of market share, and increasing difficulties competing in the global marketplace); ii) the perceived decreased effectiveness of GATT to advance its negotiating interests and objectives (as evidenced by the difficulties in concluding the protracted Uruguay Round negotiations satisfactorily and by the perception that the United States is being treated "unfairly" by its trade partners); and iii) the fear or reality of North-South partnerships in Europe and Asia cemented on trade as well as on investment flows and geared to enhance the economic restructuring of those industrial centers.

Combined with the decline of East-West confrontation, these new facts have given greater weight to economic considerations in the design of U.S. discriminatory trade policy (see Richardson, 1991, and Vernon and Spar, 1989). Neither CUSFTA nor NAFTA can be adequately understood on purely foreign policy or strategic grounds. The basic thrust of the U.S. drive toward preferential deals with its two neighbors has been economic on at least three grounds. First, by facilitating access to a new "factor mix," these arrangements (particularly NAFTA) may contribute to strengthening the competitive stance of U.S. businesses in the global marketplace (including their own domestic market). Second, by easing and eventually removing trade and investment barriers, they (again, particularly NAFTA) may enhance the benefits that will accrue to U.S. producers and investors from preferential access to (potentially) fast-growing foreign markets. Finally, as a result of their expanded coverage of issues (well beyond the realm of tariffs and trade in goods) they have set precedents in areas in which multilateral negotiations are stalled or are likely to proceed at a slower pace than U.S.-sponsored bilateral or minilateral deals.

The background against which preferential trade arrangements were revived throughout Latin America in the late 1980s also differed sharply from that of previous decades. The formerly slow and erratic movement toward export orientation has turned into a massive change of direction laid by the export imperative and the financial constraint triggered by the debt crisis of the 1980s. The legacy of depressed investment and low domestic savings rates, high debt burdens, and persistent balance of payments and fiscal constraints has, on the other hand, enhanced the marginal contribution that foreign investment can make to the resumption and sustainability of economic growth.

These new conditions and imperatives combine with—and to some extent provide an "ex-post rationale" for—the growing perception that in the present conditions of rapid technical change and far-reaching internationalization of the world economy, export and overall economic growth call for the dismantling of protection of the domestic market and for economic strategies aimed at promoting a more open and dynamic pattern of integration into the world economy. This new environment certainly helps explain the speed with which the unanimous abandonment of import-substitution industrialization has translated into far-reaching (although not necessarily sustainable) liberalization of trade regimes.[4]

Thus, in contrast to the old-fashioned goal of expanding protected domestic markets to benefit from economies of scale and specialization, the new focus of preferential liberalization in Latin America is upon improving and securing market access to facilitate industrial restructuring, and upon enhancing the attractiveness of different locations to foreign investment. The aim to strengthen each country's stance vis-à-vis a much-feared "regionalization" of the world economy also plays a leading role, as does the prospect of FTA negotiations with the United States.

II. ALLOCATIVE EFFECTS AND DYNAMIC GAINS: A SURVEY

The conventionally emphasized—and usually least important—effects of preferential trade arrangements (indeed of all trade policies) revolve around issues of resource allocation. The allocative efficiency argument maintains that, in the absence of market rigidities or imperfections, free-trade policies will promote specialization in those activities in which static comparative advantages prevail, hence maximizing economic welfare. By shifting from interventionist to free-trade policies, countries will be left with a once-and-for-all increase in economic welfare (once transition costs are accounted for) as compared to the situation previous to liberalization. The allocative-based explanation supports preferential trade liberalization as a second-best policy whenever the standard rule of trade creation being larger than trade diversion prevails.[5]

Available estimates suggest extremely modest welfare effects stemming from the reallocation of resources due to preferential trade liberalization between the United States and the Latin American countries. According to Erzan and Yeats (1992), if all U.S. tariff and "hard-core" non-tariff barriers (NTBs) were removed on a preferential basis, aggregate Latin American exports to the United States would experience a steep increase of about 8 percent (and much less as a proportion of total Latin American exports). Other direct estimates of welfare effects are more optimistic (of the order of 2 to 3 percent of 1985 GNP in the South excluding Mexico) but, interestingly, these effects stem largely from the removal of the relatively high protection levels that prevailed in Latin America in the mid-1980s rather than from enhanced market access (see Harris and Robertson, 1993).

Yet static efficiency and resource allocation arguments do not account for the whole picture and may play a relatively minor role in the overall balance of costs and benefits. Indeed, it is generally accepted that the most relevant effects of economic integration are dynamic; namely, those producing changes in the rate of economic growth through an acceleration in the rate of productivity growth and/or an increase in the rate of capital formation. The most frequently cited dynamic benefits arising out of economic integration include the effects of economies of scale, enhanced market competition and technological diffusion, diminished uncertainty and changes in the location and volume of real investments.[6]

The original Smithian case on behalf of free trade was based upon the argument that a larger market would make possible the division of labor and hence improve technical efficiency. The argument presumably applies to both export-oriented sectors and import-competing industries, to the extent that in the latter, import competition will promote a rationalization of production structures into larger productive units and, simultaneously, reduce monopolistic pricing distortions. In practice, scale economies and rationalization of production have been regarded as key contributors to the gains of economic integration, as suggested by studies on CUSFTA (Harris 1985), the effects of a unified EEC market (Baldwin, 1990) and NAFTA. (For surveys of recent studies, see Brown, 1992; Weintraub, 1992.) Although not strictly dynamic, Harris and Robertson (1993) estimate that the benefits that would accrue to the Latin American countries (excluding Mexico) from economies of scale and enhanced competition as a result of a hemispheric FTA would more than double the calculated static gains.

Technological diffusion effects can arise from enhanced trade competition, forcing domestic producers to step up the pace of technical change, as emphasized in the trade liberalization literature, and from economic cooperation in areas with significant externalities, as emphasized in the literature on regional integra-

THE NORTH-SOUTH VARIETY OF ECONOMIC INTEGRATION   9

tion in developing countries. (For a review of the role of externalities in trade and development policy, see Stewart and Ghani,
1992.) Both operate through real and pecuniary externalities and
are, in principle, relevant to the process of economic integration,
particularly of the North-South variety. When operating through
real externalities, these effects can render faster rates of economic
growth as a result of changing attitudes and motivations, a more
rapid pace of human capital formation and the promotion of
technology change and technology transfer. Pecuniary externalities, in turn, are closely related to industry interdependencies.

The effect upon real investment flows is potentially one of the
most relevant in the North-South variety of economic integration,
and it has attracted considerable attention in empirical studies and
policy statements. By reducing uncertainty regarding future trade
policies in the South and guaranteeing access to the markets of the
North, economic integration can foster a redistribution of real
investment flows among partner countries to take advantage of the
benefits of expanded markets and a new factor mix. Real investment flows from third parties can also react to discrimination,
seeking to avoid the impact of negative preferences and/or to
prevent the potential effects of increased protection in the future.
Available estimates in the case of NAFTA suggest that the effects
of increased capital mobility—interacting with scale and other
technical efficiency gains—can multiply by a factor of four the size
of static and dynamic benefits (see Brown, 1992; Ros, 1992).

One major obstacle in dealing with dynamic effects is that the
extent and direction of their impact is difficult both to grasp
ex-ante and to quantify ex-post. We may note, first, that some of
these gains (such as scale effects and technological diffusion from
enhanced competition) are not exclusive of discriminatory arrangements but intrinsic to trade liberalization in general. Yet the
literature on trade liberalization in developing countries is so full
of qualifications to the theoretical arguments presented above that
it does not lead to clear-cut conclusions. The relationship between
entrepreneurial effort and exposure to foreign competition is frag-
ile (Corden, 1974). Technological diffusion arguments rely on
specific presumptions on the relationship between market structure and productivity performance, about which the relevant literature is simply inconclusive (see Lee, 1992). Even the direction

of the empirically more tractable scale effects can be very sensitive to the modeler's assumptions on entry and exit conditions in import-competing industries, the specific demand shifts that accompany trade liberalization and the nature of competition (Rodrik, 1992; Tybout, 1992).

Some of these arguments can cut both ways, and this is why they can be and often are used to make a case for industrial protection. More precisely, they cut both ways in the sense that they warn against excessive protection as well as unhindered free trade. For the same reason, they provide less guidance in assessing the benefits and costs of moving from low or moderate levels of protection to preferential trade liberalization. The empirical literature on trade liberalization, on the other hand, does not lead to firmer conclusions, either, as a number of authors have adequately stressed (Bhagwati, 1988; Pack, 1990; Rodrik, 1992).[7]

The difficulties faced in assessing the effects on capital investments are of a different kind, but the sources of uncertainty are no less important. First, they depend on risk and uncertainty effects which, by their very nature, are extremely difficult to assess. Second, they can be very sensitive to the reference scenario, leaving a wide scope for disagreement depending on the particular assumptions made on the future of U.S. and Latin American trade policies, as well as on the evolution of the multilateral trading system. Moreover, some of the incentives for increased capital inflows will depend on the particular form adopted by regional integration schemes and the ensuing reaction of foreign investors. For example, the enforcement of rules of origin that set stringent limits for products to qualify as "regional" can effectively check some of the incentives facing third parties. However, provided preferences are large enough and the "safe haven" argument applies, investors from third parties may find it attractive to respond defensively and expand investment in the enlarged market.

These complications are compounded when large discrepancies prevail among potential partners in the levels of per-capita income. The presence of externalities derived from economies of agglomeration and the interactions between economies of scale and "natural" trade barriers (such as transport costs) open the door to cumulative processes of expansion or decay.[8] Since polarization effects may be highly relevant for economies displaying large differences in size, per-capita incomes, and levels of development, they must be taken into consideration when addressing the prospects and problems of economic integration of the North-South variety.

The ambiguities about the effects of reciprocal economic integration of the North-South variety may be illustrated by comparing the past development performance of Latin America to a rather bright future: a repetition in the Western Hemisphere of the European experience in the ten years following the establishment of the EEC. Since geographic proximity, pre-existing trade links, and the potential for intra-industry trade were more favorable to income convergence in Europe than in the Western Hemisphere, this can, indeed, be considered a best-case scenario for economic growth and income convergence across the continent.

The results of such an exercise for Brazil, Mexico, Central America and the Caribbean, and South America (excluding Brazil), are presented in Table 1. The last column in the table is based on the estimates by Harris and Robertson (1993) and shows the implications for each of the regions in terms of the rate of growth of gross domestic product (GDP) and per-capita GDP if they were to undergo an experience similar to that of the European economies after the formation of the Common Market.[9] The first two columns show the actual rates of growth in 1970–1980 and during the "lost decade" of the 1980s.

Two results emerge from the table. First, a "European scenario" would imply a dramatic and positive turnaround in comparison to the growth performance of the crisis years of the 1980s. Yet it is surprising and interesting to note that even under these optimistic assumptions, it would not involve a clear improvement of growth performance as compared to the pre-crisis period, at least for the then-fastest growing Latin American countries (Brazil and Mexico, accounting for over half of the region's population). For these two countries, the growth rate of per-capita incomes in 1970–80 either falls within the projected range (Mexico) or exceeds it (Brazil); and in both cases, projected GDP growth is clearly below the GDP growth performance of the 1970s.

Surely, a comparison of this "European scenario" with the growth performance before 1980 may seem inappropriate, as a repetition of the experience of the fastest growing economies in

Table 1
A "European Scenario" Compared

| | Annual rates of growth | | | | | |
| | 1970–1980 | | 1980–1990 | | 1995–2006 | |
	GDP	GDP per capita	GDP	GDP per capita	GDP	GDP per capita
Brazil	8.6	6.1	1.6	−0.6	5.8–7.3	4.3–5.8
Mexico	6.5	3.4	1.6	−0.7	4.9–6.1	3.4–4.6
Rest of South America	3.1	0.8	0.7	−1.4	6.2–7.9	4.6–6.3
Central America & Caribbean	4.3	1.8	0.7	−1.7	8.1–10.4	6.2–8.4
Latin America	5.6	3.1	1.2	−0.9		

Sources: Harris and Robertson (1993); ECLAC (1991)

the region may well be very unlikely under any plausible circumstances. But so is the implicit comparison with the European experience before integration (see note 9), given the very different pre-integration trends toward income convergence in Europe and Latin America. At the same time, it is clear that any positive degree of income convergence would imply a substantial improvement over the trends of the past decade.

This cursory examination of the dynamic effects of reciprocal economic integration of the North-South variety leads to the conclusion that traditional theory and empirical evidence do not provide straightforward answers about their size and direction. The balance of dynamic effects will ultimately rest upon the uncertain balance of "virtuous" as opposed to "vicious" circles of investment, productivity, and growth, about which economic analysis provides all but precise answers.[10] In practice, economic structure and localization issues will interplay to give rise eventually to contrasting outcomes between countries able to create "growth poles" or virtuous circles of growth and investment, as opposed to decadence.

III. Structure of Incentives in Latin America

Although existing theoretical arguments and empirical evidence do not allow for clear-cut conclusions, they may be of greater help in assessing how the potential net gains from North-South integration may be distributed among the Latin American countries. In this case, they are also useful in examining the structure of incentives each country will face under the prospect of such economic integration and, particularly, the heterogeneous nature of their policy dilemmas.

We will follow an approach to this issue that differs from other assessments emphasizing the stylized conclusions stemming from allocative arguments. By definition, they beg the dilemmas posed by uncertain net benefits and transition costs associated with trade liberalization. Analytically, the effects of North-South discriminatory trade liberalization for each of the Latin American countries are the result of three overlapping influences: i) a unilateral import liberalization component (i.e., the reduction or elimination of protection for domestic producers); ii) the improved and more secure market access derived from the removal of tariff and NTBs on exports to the United States and from the lock-in of these changes; and iii) a trade diversion component, to the extent that the preferences granted to the United States are not extended to other trading partners. The last two components are specific to discriminatory liberalization, whereas the first one is intrinsic to any form of trade liberalization.

Standard assessments of the distribution of net gains among Latin American countries evaluate the benefits from the first two components (the efficiency gains resulting from reciprocal trade liberalization) and compare them to the welfare losses associated to the third one (the trade diversion effects arising from remaining protection vis-à-vis the rest of the world). In these exercises, the counterfactual experiment (economic integration with the United States) is compared to the status quo, taken to be existing levels of protection in different countries. This approach emphasizes the uncertain results of preferential trade liberalization stemming from the traditional "trade diversion" versus "trade creation" criteria, but generally begs the ambiguities of the relevant literature on trade liberalization.

Therefore, it may be more useful to our discussion to follow an alternative two-step procedure. First, we will briefly review the balance of benefits and costs that result from the market access and trade diversion effects faced by each country (i.e., the net benefits arising from the second and third components of economic integration). In doing so, we assume away the existing levels of import protection in the Latin American countries and, therefore, take as the reference scenario not the status quo but, rather, one of full and unilateral trade liberalization in the South. It can easily be confirmed that in this imaginary scenario, the gains from market access and the costs from trade diversion fully and unambiguously determine the distribution of gains across the region. Later on we will bring into the analysis the effects of the unilateral import liberalization component of economic integration upon the incentives structure.

This procedure, awkward as it may seem, has the advantage over the conventional approach of isolating the ambiguities of preferential trade liberalization with respect to both the preferential and the trade liberalization components of economic integration. Given the sizable differences in regional and commodity trade patterns, economic structures and localization advantages throughout Latin America, the preferential components by themselves give rise to a fairly heterogeneous structure of incentives across the region. The uncertainty and transitional issues posed by the liberalization component further illustrate the contrasting nature of the policy dilemmas faced by the Latin American countries.

Allocative Gains

For the Latin American countries, net static benefits of preferential trade liberalization vis-à-vis the United States will be positively correlated with the degree to which the United States is a "natural" trading partner, and the extent to which the Latin American country's exports face tariff and ("removable") NTBs in the U.S. market. They will also be inversely correlated with the size of preferences granted to the United States (i.e., remaining protection vis-à-vis the rest of the world). The first and second determine the extent of trade creation, while the first and third influence the room for trade diversion.

A rule of thumb suggests that, at comparable levels of re-maining protection, the more a country trades with the United States relative to third partners and the higher the share of man-ufactures in its exports to the United States, the larger the net benefits of preferential trade liberalization vis-à-vis its northern neighbor.[11] In purely static terms, high trade concentration in the U.S. market implies limited room for welfare losses stemming from trade diversion. In the same vein, and given that most Latin American primary exports face zero or low barriers, a high share of manufactures in total exports to the United States suggests a large potential to benefit from the removal of trade barriers in sectors where they hurt most (Erzan and Yeats, 1992).

Since regional and commodity trade patterns as well as trade regimes differ considerably, this set of factors brings forth a fairly heterogeneous structure of incentives throughout the region. This diversity is shown in Figure 1, where four groups of countries can be distinguished according to the extent and nature of their trade relations with the United States (and Canada): i) "natural" trading partner exporters of manufactures (Mexico and Caricom); ii) "natural" trading partner exporters of primary products (Central America, Colombia, Venezuela, Ecuador); iii) diversified exporters of manufactures (Brazil, Argentina, Paraguay, and Uruguay—the Mercosur countries); and iv) diversified exporters of primary products (Bolivia, Chile, Peru).

The unequal distribution of market access gains can be illus-trated with the estimates of the impact of removing U.S. trade barriers (both tariff and NTBs) on Latin American exports pro-vided by Erzan and Yeats (1992) (in Figure 1 the estimates are shown in parentheses as percentages of total 1987/88 exports). These estimates confirm the primary role of regional trade patterns in determining the potential for export expansion and explain why the largest gains (relative to total exports) accrue to Mexico, Central America, and the Caribbean countries, which display the highest U.S. trade concentration ratios. Figure 1 also highlights the role that the nature of trade links plays in determining the scope for gains stemming from increased access to the U.S. market. The importance of U.S. trade barriers in manufacturing and the com-modity composition of trade account for the fact that the gains for some countries that are predominantly exporters of manufactures

Figure 1
Trade Concentration Ratios

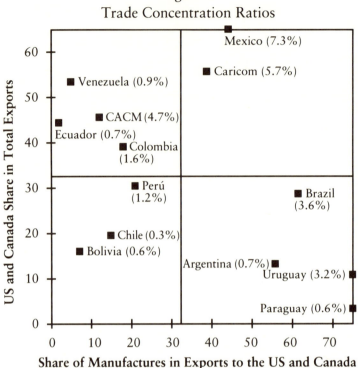

Source: Erzan and Yeats (1992); Trade Concentration Ratios Based on UN COMTRADE Data Base, 1987 and 1988.

to the United States (such as Brazil or Uruguay) are much higher than those reaped by "natural" U.S. trading partners that are primary exporters (such as Venezuela or Ecuador).

Dynamic Effects

Net dynamic benefits—stemming from economies of scale, technological diffusion and investment effects—are also bound to be unequally distributed across Latin America. Differences in economic structure, along with localization, regional trade patterns, and country size, are here likely to play a major role. At comparable economic size, the impact of scale effects resulting from access to larger markets will be positively correlated with: i) the importance of the manufacturing sector in the overall economy (where economies of scale are likely to exist and where relatively higher U.S. trade barriers prevail); and ii) the scope of intra-industry trade, which allows for further rationalization effects and gains from specialization.

A similar reasoning can be applied to technological diffusion and investment effects. Technological diffusion, operating through real and pecuniary externalities—which are in turn closely related to industry interdependencies—are likely to be of more limited relevance for natural resource-based economies than for semi-industrialized countries where some activities subject to rapid technological change already exist or may be more easily established. The potential to mobilize new flows of real investment is also likely to be closely associated to the ability of individual countries to engage in intra-industry trade and specialization. It is likely that countries with a large share of foreign direct investment in primary sectors have already reaped a large share of the opportunities for specialization along the lines of static comparative advantages.[12]

Economic size introduces an additional factor, but one with a role far from unambiguous. In principle, some of the major potential dynamic gains would be particularly relevant for countries with small domestic markets. Having access to a large market may contribute to reaping the benefits of scale economies and support technical efficiency. Yet to the extent that their small markets are the consequence of low per-capita incomes, these countries are likely to be less industrialized and to have foreign trade structures that are predominantly inter-industry in character, therefore limiting the potential to reap the benefits of scale effects.[13] In practice, there is a strong correlation between the degree of industrialization and the level of per-capita incomes across the region and, to some extent, also between market size and intra-industry trade. At least, the larger economies are all among the more industrialized countries in the region and are clearly the leaders in terms of intra-industry specialization.

Protection and the Structure of Incentives

Our analysis of the distribution of net gains across Latin America has so far ignored the benefits and costs of the unilateral import liberalization component of North-South integration. Such an assumption is inadequate and removes from the analysis what some regard as the major benefit of hemispheric integration and others view as a major source of potential trouble. As we shall see, this component, in practice, makes a large contribution to the understanding of some political economy issues taken up later in the paper.

Two questions are relevant with regard to the unilateral liberalization component: a) How are differences in existing levels of protection across countries likely to affect the incentives for economic integration? and b) What differential effects among countries may be expected from an equal reduction in import protection? Again, economic analysis offers unambiguous answers only in the limited realm of static effects and allocative issues.

As regards the first, high-protection countries would stand to benefit considerably more from trade liberalization than low-protection ones. This is clearly shown by estimates by Harris and Robertson (1993), where the welfare gains of hemispheric integration across the region are largely determined by the size of the reduction in tariffs, and thus accrue mostly to those countries with the highest pre-existing levels of protection. As regards the second, and given that the static costs of protection are inversely related to market size, small countries would stand to gain more than large ones from an equal reduction of protection. In this logic, the gains from the unilateral import liberalization component of economic integration would accrue mostly to the small and highly protected economies and diminish as we move toward the large and more liberalized countries.

These answers, and the resulting structure of incentives, turn out to be counterintuitive. Since under conventional assumptions high-protection countries are those that would benefit most from economic integration (in fact, from trade liberalization), we would find Brazil and Colombia among the most enthusiastic advocates of FTA agreements with the United States. In contrast, low-protection countries such as Mexico or Chile would stand to receive limited gains. It is interesting to note that Mexico's interest would rank low by both criteria.

This distribution of incentives will be altered if dynamic effects are taken into consideration. Again, potential costs may be much larger in small economies as the risks of adverse polarization effects may increase with reduced market size. Wide differences in per-capita incomes across Latin America (of the order of 10 to 1 between the richest and the poorest countries), and the potential interactions among the different sources of dynamic benefits, raises as an important issue the prospect of vicious circles in the smaller and poorer countries of the region. Similarly, large and (moderately) protected economies should be careful in implementing trade liberalization due to the uncertain dynamic effects surveyed in Section II. Furthermore, the import liberalization component gives rise to the extremely relevant issue of transition costs which, if not addressed explicitly, can obscure the nature of the policy dilemmas faced by the individual countries.

Transition Costs and Macroeconomic Constraints

Exercises in comparative statics can beg the issue of transition costs because these can be accommodated if the final outcome renders a net benefit. From a policy-relevant discussion, however, this misses two key issues: the intertemporal distribution of costs and benefits, and the fact that because unilateral trade liberalization is always available as a policy option, its benefits can be "unilaterally" reaped. Both of these suggest that potential and effective (transitional) costs are likely to play a major role in each country's weighting of overall costs and benefits,[14] and they explain why leaving them aside can easily lead to counterintuitive results.

One area that will heavily influence transition costs (and therefore the sustainability of trade liberalization) is the macroeconomic environment, as import liberalization will generally alter the conditions required to achieve or maintain internal and external balance. In fact, one lesson drawn from experience is that, besides the more or less positive legacy of past industrialization strategies, the transitional costs and sustainability of trade liberalization policies are closely related to the ability to effectively respond to these macroeconomic changes.

In the absence of compensating capital movements, maintaining external and internal balance will require trade liberalization to be accompanied by real depreciation of the domestic currency.[15] Even if the foreign exchange constraint is not binding, real depreciation can have an important role in policy sustainability. By providing "implicit" protection to producers for the domestic market and increasing exporters' benefits (consequently easing adjustment costs and acting as a deterrent to the formation of coalitions opposed to trade liberalization), real depreciation may contribute to policy sustainability.[16]

The implications of real depreciation—and the ability to achieve it—will vary greatly depending on the degree of macroeconomic stability of the domestic economy, the fiscal effects of devaluation, and the extent of the liberalization exercise as compared to the pre-existing levels of protection. Its consequences have been mostly discussed in the context of countries facing large domestic macroeconomic imbalances and have focused on policy trade-offs between macroeconomic stabilization (which calls for a low exchange rate) and trade liberalization (which calls for a high exchange rate). The presence of fiscal effects from devaluation—which can actually be more important than the direct fiscal consequences of import liberalization—further complicates the picture. Their size and direction largely depend on the state of the public sector's foreign-exchange balance, i.e., approximately the difference between government export revenues (from taxes or public ownership of primary exports) and net transfer payments on public external debt. Since the required size of devaluation depends on pre-existing levels of protection, taking all these factors together determines a diversity of national situations, leaving high-protection countries that simultaneously face domestic macroeconomic instability and potentially destabilizing effects from devaluation in the most vulnerable position.[17]

Potentially, the effects of prospective trade agreements on capital movements can help soften these trade-offs. The Mexican experience after 1988 has, in fact, been one of trade liberalization with real appreciation whose sustainability has been made possible by massive capital inflows, partly resulting from the prospect of NAFTA being established. Yet these effects should be regarded as a mixed blessing, rather than a straightforward benefit. A puzzling situation could develop in which the prospects of an FTA could raise favorable expectations and stimulate capital inflows, thereby reinforcing real exchange-rate misalignments. Paradoxically, the more favorable the expectations of financial markets, the larger the potential exchange-rate misalignment from the point of view of adjustment costs and the long-term sustainability of the liberalization process.[18] We may also note that in the Mexican experience alluded to above, capital inflows and real appreciation followed a period (from 1985 to late 1987) in which the "initial shock" of import liberalization had been greatly softened by a high real exchange rate.[19] The initial and substantial margin of currency undervaluation also provided exchange-rate policy with an enlarged room to maneuver in the face of the subsequent turnaround of the capital account after 1989.

The previous discussion underlines the importance and the problems of "getting the exchange rate right" at the time of entry into an agreement and some of the challenges facing exchange-rate management in the post-liberalization period. The desirable dose of real exchange-rate flexibility will also be influenced by other factors. The prospect of a more stable real exchange rate may enhance the potential to reap the benefits of less uncertainty and capital market integration. However, real exchange-rate stability vis-à-vis the strong-currency partner will imply that the effective real exchange rate will be residually determined by the strong-currency partner's exchange-rate policies. This may give rise to policy dilemmas in countries with regionally diversified trade and investment patterns.

IV. POLITICAL ECONOMY ISSUES AND PATH-DEPENDENT OUTCOMES

In Section III we emphasized the structure of incentives arising from the market access and trade discrimination components of North-South integration, qualified to take into account the effects of import liberalization. Except for the discussion on transition costs, this was to a large extent an exercise in comparative statics, useful in showing the heterogeneous structure of incentives prevailing across the region. Yet precisely because of this heterogeneity, economic integration in the Western Hemisphere will not be achieved in a one-shot movement.

Thus the interactions between alternative scenarios and ensuing processes will heavily influence final outcomes. In other words, the structure of incentives is highly sensitive (and will correspondingly change) with the assumed reference scenario. Yet the relevant reference scenario will itself change as a result of the actions emerging from a given structure of incentives. As a result, the perceived evolution of regional (and multilateral) arrangements as well as emerging deals regarding "entry fees" and the distribution of costs and benefits will provide the background against which "positive incentives" will operate. Actions emerging from these incentives will, in turn, affect the actual evolution of trade arrangements, opening the door for path-dependent outcomes.

"Defensive" Motivations and Costs of Exclusion

One source of "defensive" motivations for trade discrimination is the willingness to gain "insurance" against mounting protectionist practices in other countries' markets. This incentive will be positively related to the importance of the partners' market as an export outlet and to the strength of prevailing protectionist tides. Its value will depend on how much insurance against procedural or other forms of protectionism an agreement can effectively provide. Although Mexican and Canadian negotiators had to waive their original expectations, the search for more stable and predictable market access has been frequently offered as an explanation for the Mexican and Canadian drives toward free-trade arrangements with the United States.[20]

Another source of defensive motivations may be the desire to avoid the costs of negative discrimination as a result of third-party actions. These costs relate to the beggar-thy-neighbor component of preferential trade arrangements, i.e., that they may increase participants' welfare at the expense of the rest of the world. The incentive to engage in such defensive actions (including the attempt to become a member of the arrangement) will be dependent upon the strength of the effects of trade diversion, investment diversion, and deterioration in the terms of trade. Other things being equal, the overall potential for trade and investment diversion and negative terms of trade effects will be positively related to the margin of preferences exchanged by countries entering into the agreement and their prominence as trade and investment partners for third countries. Although its importance is not uniform throughout the region, the United States is one of the largest markets and sources of foreign direct investment for most Latin American countries. As a result, one would expect that discriminatory arrangements of the North-South variety would heavily influence attitudes and reactions in a wide spectrum of countries in the Western Hemisphere.

So far, analysis of this issue has focused on the trade and investment diversion effects of NAFTA. One examination of available empirical estimates concludes that "the overall impact of NAFTA on the rest of the world should not be significant if the agreement fosters freer trade among its participants" (Primo Braga, 1992). This conclusion is supported by partial equilibrium analysis, which shows a very limited impact of NAFTA upon U.S. imports from the rest of the world. In particular, the effects on Latin American exports to the U.S. market are very small—a contraction of less than 0.1 percent (Erzan and Yeats, 1992)—with most of the impact being felt outside the Western Hemisphere. The results of computable general equilibrium models (CGE) do not suggest a large impact (either negative or positive) upon the rest of the world (ROW).[21] Attempts to grasp the impact of NAFTA's "growth dividend" upon the ROW do not render large effects, either (for a discussion, see Primo Braga, 1992).

In closer scrutiny, however, these exercises do not provide solid grounds for concluding that defensive motivations would consequently be negligible. First, available knowledge provides uncertain answers as to how small these effects will actually be. Although they are helpful analytical tools, the limits of static partial equilibrium exercises are well known. CGE studies also lead to less straightforward conclusions than might be inferred by the inattentive reader. Two lessons drawn from available exercises seem particularly appropriate at this point: i) that even the direction of effects upon the ROW is uncertain due to the large dependence of conclusions from underlying assumptions and basic behavioral relationships, and ii) that capital flows and the shape of the agreements play a key role in determining the effect of discriminatory arrangements upon the ROW. Precarious knowledge about the determinants of investment and the variety of factors that can influence the size of investment diversion effects render an uncertain outcome in a particularly critical area (see Collins, 1992).

Furthermore, although the overall effect upon trade and investment flows may be modest, for some individual countries and particular economic activities the consequences could be very significant.[22] Even if average tariff protection in countries engaging in discriminatory arrangements is low (as in the case of the United States), NTBs and contingent protection can be relevant in producing trade diversion effects for individual products. This can be particularly true if discriminatory arrangements take the form of managed trade, as it seems to have happened with NAFTA at least in the case of agriculture, textiles and apparel, and automobiles.

Therefore, the standard conclusion that the overall effects of NAFTA on third countries are likely to be small should not be taken as implying that defensive motivations in the Western Hemisphere may not turn out to be important determinants of policy response. Concerns clearly exist and reactions have not been mute in Latin America. Some countries (such as those from Central America and the Caribbean) have expressed misgivings about the fact that, if no action is taken, NAFTA will involve an erosion of existing preferences. Other countries fear the potential effects of negative discrimination. It is likely, as Primo Braga (1992) maintains, that some countries have refrained from expressing their concerns because they lack other alternatives or because they expect soon to become members of North-South discriminatory arrangements in the Western Hemisphere and would therefore share in the benefits from which they are so far excluded.

In any case, and beyond the issue of the specific quantitative effects of NAFTA on other countries, the costs of exclusion will mount over time as the number of participants increase. So far, most concerns regarding the effects of negative discrimination have been related to the U.S. market. However, as other countries that are more active participants in intra-Latin American trade are eventually incorporated into North-South agreements, the issue of trade diversion will transcend the U.S. market and impinge upon intra-Latin American trade flows as well. This may turn out to be a powerful defensive motivation for countries that have "natural" trade partnerships with neighbor countries (i.e., the Southern Cone countries).

The costs of exclusion will also be dependent upon the effectiveness of the rules and institutions governing the multilateral trading system. As effective multilateral arrangements are likely to erode the margin of preferences exchanged by discriminatory partners, they will reduce—yet not eliminate—the costs to those being left out. If a scenario of trade fragmentation gradually evolves, the costs for those excluded will mount correspondingly, even if the discriminating partners do not raise protection vis-à-vis the ROW. Irrespective of whether such fragmentation takes the form of closer trade and investment relations among "natural trade partners" (and consequently do not involve a large component of trade diversion), countries left behind may suffer considerably (Krugman, 1991). Various Latin American countries, particularly in the Southern Cone, stand among the most likely candidates to be adversely affected by such a scenario. Since discriminatory trade policies can also contribute to the fragmentation of multilateral arrangements, the costs of which will be unevenly distributed among countries, the importance of systemic implications can hardly be overemphasized.

Distribution of Costs and Benefits, Costs of Exclusion, and Entry Fees

"Side payments" and entry fees will influence the likelihood and shape the content of hemispheric integration. Their nature then becomes a critical issue for the Latin American countries and the prospects of North-South integration in the Western Hemisphere.

A side payment or an entry fee to engage in economic discrimination can be explained on two grounds. First, it can be seen as a reparation for the unequal distribution of costs and benefits among partners of different size. To the extent that the large country's prices will dominate the post-integration structure of relative prices, the small partner stands to benefit relatively more from the effects of integration of resource allocation. This will lead the larger partner to demand additional concessions in order to enter into an agreement (Dixit, 1987).[23] Second, the side payment can be viewed as a compensation to avoid the costs of exclusion on the part of those left behind. As far as the latter is concerned, it is clear that entry fees will tend to increase with the costs of exclusion and the intensity of defensive motivations.

As mentioned in Section I, one of the characteristics of "new vintage" discriminatory arrangements (particularly of the North-South variety) is that their agenda and coverage extend well beyond the realm of tariff barriers and trade in goods. Since the early 1980s, U.S. policy has successfully included in trade negotiations a set of (then) new issues that stretched out beyond the traditional agenda. At its core, it included the establishment of a common framework to deal with trade in services, foreign investment regulations, and protection of intellectual property rights. The United States was successful in introducing these issues into the negotiating agenda of the Uruguay Round. At the time, they were seen as the counterpart for opening developed countries' agricultural and textile markets in the global deal offered to the developing world.

While the protracted state of multilateral trade negotiations makes these issues obvious candidates to extract side payments in exchange for enlarged access to the U.S. market, two factors turn them into not-so-new issues in the hemispheric context and, therefore, reduce their value as side payments from the standpoint of the United States. First, the divergence of negotiating and policy objectives between the United States and most Latin American countries has shrunk remarkably in recent years, as a result of changes in Latin America's economic strategies, U.S. "aggressive unilateralism" (section 301, "super" 301), and international financial institutions' conditionality. Second, provided a pessimistic scenario about the final outcome of the Uruguay Round of trade negotiations does not prevail, it is likely that the preliminary agreements already bargained for in the multilateral arena eventually will be brought into operation.

Yet with the United States as the *demandeur*, any bilateral or minilateral agreement will go beyond what may eventually emerge from a multilateral deal.[24] From a Latin American standpoint, it therefore remains extremely important to assess the significance of any "incremental" outcome likely to emerge from bilateral or minilateral as compared to multilateral deals. Not-so-new issues involve sensitive areas where developing and developed countries' interests and policies can diverge substantially.[25] Consequently, a delicate policy trade-off may be involved.

The recent inclusion in NAFTA negotiations of a brand-new set of issues that go beyond trade in services, investment regulations, and intellectual property rights, indicates the superior bargaining position of the United States. The brand-new issues include concerns for environmental, labor, and sanitary standards, all of which now occupy a prominent role in negotiations and domestic debates. This bodes poorly for the prospect of hemispheric integration as these issues likely will meet strong disagreement stemming from varying levels of national development, and from differing societal practices and preferences. The explicit or implicit loss of national autonomy in policy design, as a result of arbitrage among widely different national institutions and practices, can be very significant. In such conditions, institutional convergence becomes more difficult and not necessarily more desirable.[26]

Brand-New Issues, Adjustment Costs, and the "Political Economy Gap"

If a discriminatory arrangement improves its members' welfare, it is unambiguously beneficial. This textbook conclusion, however, leaves a major practical issue unresolved: How are transition costs to be dealt with? From a political economy standpoint, transition costs cannot be omitted from the analysis, particularly if they are unequally distributed among partners. In practice, due to the peculiarities of the U.S.-Latin American bargaining structure, it is likely that a "political economy gap" will emerge between the way in which costs are effectively distributed among partners and the way in which partners are compensated.

To begin with, and as stressed by standard trade theory, the counterpart of larger efficiency gains by the smaller partner is a larger reallocation of resources and higher dislocation costs.[27] These will be higher the more protected the economy is and the more structural rigidities exist (such as imperfect price/wage flexibility or specific factors of production). Adjustment costs will also be influenced by macroeconomic and exchange-rate policies. It is likely that all these factors, given the conditions prevailing in many Latin American countries and referred to in Section III, will tend to make the transitional problems far more difficult to tackle in the South than in the North.

However, perceptions arising from the political economy of negotiations can be far removed from the way in which actual adjustment costs are likely to be distributed between South and North. This political economy gap arises from another asymmetry between small and large partners. In the smaller partner, and in contrast to unilateral liberalization, trade discrimination will tend to stimulate the formation of coalitions in favor of liberalization prompted by their interest in obtaining access to the larger country's market.[28] These coalitions can balance the influence of those negatively affected by preferential trade liberalization, therefore improving the odds of policies to succeed and limiting the need to devise policies to compensate for the costs of adjustment. In the larger country, instead, sectors negatively affected by trade liberalization are likely to be more vocal than those benefiting from market access to the small country's market. This tendency will be reinforced if the eventual losers in the small country are structurally weaker in the political arena than their counterparts in the larger country, as is the case in many Latin American countries.[29]

These arguments can help explain why policies for dealing with adjustment costs are likely to receive more attention and resources in the larger country than in the smaller one. Going one step further, one may suggest that the prominence acquired by the brand-new issues in NAFTA negotiations, indicating what other partners in the line may expect, can be partly interpreted as a result of this political economy gap. So far the issue of transition costs has attracted much more attention in the North than in the South.

The political economy gap that currently dominates public perceptions regarding adjustment costs can become a serious obstacle to establishing much needed mechanisms to deal with undesirable distributive outcomes.[30] Even more, by focusing attention on the adjustment costs faced by the North—where they are likely to be less serious and more easily dealt with—the gap between perceptions and realities could pose a formidable political obstacle to negotiation and implementation.

V. Concluding Remarks

Irrespective of whether countries other than Mexico engage in North-South negotiations in the near future, the sole fact of NAFTA being implemented will influence the scenario and the perceived options on the part of other countries in the region. It is therefore appropriate to review the emerging policy issues Latin American countries are likely to face as a result. This paper dealt with some of these issues. In doing so, we have deliberately questioned some of the more optimistic assessments of the North-South variety of economic integration and brought attention to some problems that have so far been neglected.

We began by noting that "new vintage" trade discrimination in the Western Hemisphere differs considerably from approaches typical of previous decades. On the U.S. side, trade discrimination is no longer implemented mainly for purposes of security and/or foreign policy (although these factors may still play a role). Rather, an economic rationale for trade discrimination can now be found in the prevailing dissatisfaction with the GATT regime, and in the need to enhance global competitiveness in a context of decreasing economic and technological leadership. On the Latin American side, trade discrimination is having a new chance against a background of trade liberalization and enhanced awareness of the need to promote a more effective integration into the world economy.

Our survey of analytical arguments and available empirical evidence with regard to the static and dynamic effects of North-South discrimination in the Western Hemisphere was inconclusive. There is widespread agreement that allocative effects are generally small, except for the Latin American countries in which protection is highest. Yet this consensus brings no certainty: The fact that dynamic effects are far more relevant in determining the net benefits of North-South economic integration opens new roads to indeterminacy. In effect, many of the dynamic arguments that can be used on behalf of preferential liberalization (such as economies of scale or real externalities) are also applicable on behalf of moderate and transitory protection. The extent to which foreign investment will react is also uncertain, given the imprecise knowledge about its overall determinants. This ambiguous response is

aggravated when large disparities of income and levels of development prevail, since they increase the potential for polarization
effects—that is to say, to cumulative processes of expansion or
decay.

Despite this indeterminacy, theoretical arguments and empirical evidence are more helpful in assessing how the potential net
gains from North-South integration may be distributed among the
Latin American countries. The straightforward conclusion is that
the emerging structure of incentives will be highly heterogeneous
across the region. Our analysis focused on the three effects in
which discriminatory liberalization could be analytically decom-
posed. This showed that available estimates of the distribution of
net benefits from hemispheric integration across Latin America
ignored the ambiguities derived from the component of unilateral
import liberalization in the context of North-South economic
integration and begged the crucial issue of transition costs. Transition costs stand as a critical factor, particularly in the macroeconomic environment prevailing in most of Latin America.

Yet it is interesting to note that whichever the balance of
benefits and costs, the structure of incentives will be highly sensitive to the assumed reference scenario. The latter, in turn, will
change on behalf of actions induced by those perceived incentives
and by the evolution of multilateral arrangements. This being so,
motivations of a more defensive character can radically alter the
balance of incentives across countries. They may also influence
the height of entry fees and, consequently, the distribution of costs
and benefits among participating countries, in turn affecting incentives to negotiate. The rise in costs of exclusion and the prospect of increasing entry fees can become a powerful force in favor
of expanding the negotiations, but they can also become a source
of resentment in the hemisphere and lead to sour economic and
political relations.

The new issues, which looked like promising candidates for
the role of side payments and/or entry fees, are now being joined
by the brand-new issues of environmental, labor, and sanitary
standards. The prominence of these brand-new issues reflects
the concern in the North for adjustment costs, which so far has
attracted much more attention than the transitional problems of

the South. Yet, as we have argued, the latter are likely to be far more difficult to tackle than the former. This political economy gap between how costs are distributed and how they are being addressed is rooted in the asymmetries between domestic coalitions in the North and South. This may become, however, a formidable political obstacle to successful negotiation and implementation of future agreements.

Appendix 1
Preferential Trade Agreements in the Western Hemisphere

Name and Membership	Date	Objective
LATIN AMERICAN INTEGRATION ASSOCIATION (LAIA): all Spanish-speaking South American countries, Mexico, and Brazil	1980	Established as a result of the failure to achieve the objectives set by the Latin American Free Trade Association (LAFTA) in 1960. *Objectives:* To gradually achieve a common market. *Instruments:* Area of economic preferences constituted by regional tariff preferences, regional agreements and partial agreements (economic complementation, agricultural and/or trade promoting agreements).
CENTRAL AMERICAN COMMON MARKET (CACM): Costa Rica, Guatemala, Honduras, El Salvador, and Nicaragua.	1960	*Objective:* To establish a common market in 1965.
CARIBBEAN COMMUNITY (Caricom): Jamaica, St. Cristobal, Dominica, St. Vincent, Antigua, Barbados, Guyana, Belize, Granada, St. Lucia, Trinidad & Tobago, Monserrat, and Bahamas	1973	*Objectives:* To create a common market regime in order to strengthen, coordinate and regulate trade and economic relations among members. In 1990 member countries reformulated the objectives and set December 1991 as the deadline to establish a common external tariff.

Current Status	Memoranda (1990)
All member countries have signed bilateral agreements exchanging preferences for predetermined lists of products. A number of member countries have signed economic complementation agreements. Recent economic complementation agreements include those signed by Argentina-Chile (1990), Mexico-Honduras (1990), Chile-Venezuela (1990), Bolivia-Uruguay (1991), Chile-Mexico (1991), El Salvador-Honduras (1992), Guatemala-El Salvador (1992), Guatemala-Honduras (1992). The nonextension to other members of preferences granted by Mexico to imports from Canada and the US under NAFTA will demand a reform, a waiver, or a sanction under the terms of the Montevideo Treaty.	Aggregate GDP: US$863.5 billion Population: 380 million Total foreign trade: US$202.4 billion Intra-regional trade as percentage of total foreign trade: 10.3
In 1991 member countries made the commitment to establish a common external tariff (5–20%) by January 1993. Due to their failure to meet the targets El Salvador, Guatemala, and Honduras agreed to establish a free-trade area by January 1993 (see below).	Aggregate GDP: US$25.6 billion Population: 26.2 million Total foreign trade: US$11.5 billion Intra-regional trade as percentage of total foreign trade: 5.7
Due to the failure to meet the calendar, a new deadline (1994) to establish a common market was set.	Aggregate GDP: US$28.2 billion Population: 9.4 million Total foreign trade: US$12.4 billion Intra-regional trade as percentage of total foreign trade: 3.0

Name and Membership	Date	Objective
ANDEAN GROUP: Bolivia, Colombia, Ecuador, Peru, and Venezuela	1969	*Objective:* To promote harmonious development of member countries and the gradual formation of a Latin American common market. *Instruments:* Harmonization of social and economic policies, joint programs, liberalization program, and minimum common external tariff. In 1991, a new date (1–1–92) was set to establish a common market.
CANADA–UNITED STATES FREE TRADE AGREEMENT (CUSFTA)	1988	*Objective:* To establish a free-trade area in January 1998. Some tariffs and quotas will be eliminated immediately, but most will be phased out in five to ten years in annual installments. *Major exceptions:* agricultural quotas, price support and subsidy programs of both countries. Canadian regulations on beer, books, video and audio recording and government procurement not covered by GATT. The agreement phases out within three years most of the screening requirements to investments. US banks and insurance companies will enjoy much greater market access. Almost all existing restrictions on trade in non-financial services—which are excluded from the agreement—are grandfathered.
SOUTHERN COMMON MARKET (Mercosur): Argentina, Brazil, Uruguay, and Paraguay	1991	*Objective:* To establish a common market by 1–1–95. *Instruments:* Commercial liberalization program, macroeconomic policy coordination, common external tariff, sectoral agreements.
CHILE-MEXICO FREE TRADE AGREEMENT	1991	*Objective:* To establish a free-trade area by 1–1–96.

Current Status	Memoranda (1990)
The date was not met due to internal disagreements. In 1992 Peru suspended its tariff preferences. A new common tariff was negotiated and a transition period was set until December 1993. Colombia and Venezuela negotiated a bilateral free-trade agreement (see below).	Aggregate GDP: US$130.9 billion Population: 91.2 million Total foreign trade: US$47.3 billion Intra-regional trade as percentage of total foreign trade: 3.8
Signed and ratified by US Congress and Canadian Parliament.	Aggregate GDP: US$5,990 billion Population: 276.5 million Total foreign trade: US$1,161 billion Intra-regional trade as percentage of total foreign trade: 34.0
Present tariff preferences: 68% Dispute Resolution Agreement signed. Products are being gradually removed from national lists of exclusion as planned. Common external tariff will be announced in June 1993.	Aggregate GDP: US$492.3 billion Population: 190 million Total foreign trade: US$76.3 billion Intra-regional trade as percentage of total foreign trade: 8.6
Present maximum reciprocal tariff: 7.5%	Aggregate GDP: US$240.2 billion Population: 99.4 million Total foreign trade: US$78.8 billion Intra-regional trade as percentage of total foreign trade: 0.1

Name and Membership	Date	Objective
COLOMBIA-VENEZUELA FREE TRADE AGREEMENT	1992	*Objective:* To establish a free-trade area by 1992.
GROUP OF 3: COLOMBIA-VENEZUELA-MEXICO FREE TRADE AGREEMENT	1993	*Objective:* Economic cooperation. In April 1993, the three countries agreed to establish a free-trade area by 1994.
CHILE-VENEZUELA FREE TRADE AGREEMENT	1993	*Objective:* To establish a free-trade area by 1999.
NUEVA OCOTEPEQUE AGREEMENT: (El Salvador, Honduras, and Guatemala)	1992	*Objective:* To establish a free-trade area by 1993. Long-run objective: to establish a customs union. Includes recent economic complementation agreements signed among these countries
MEXICO, COSTA RICA–EL SALVADOR–GUATEMALA-HONDURAS-NICARAGUA FREE TRADE AGREEMENT	1992	*Objective:* To establish a free-trade area by 31–12–96.
U.S.A.-MEXICO-CANADA FREE TRADE AGREEMENT (NAFTA)	1992	*Objective:* To create a free-trade area by 2009. Elimination of tariffs in five, ten, or fifteen years depending on the type of product. Exceptions are to Canadian agricultural and Mexican petroleum products. The agreement contains precedent-setting rights and obligations regarding intellectual-property rights, services, trade, and investment. NAFTA extends the Canada-US Free Trade Agreement dispute settlement system to Mexico in return for trade law revisions that will align Mexican administrative practices more closely to US-Canadian norms.

Current Status	Memoranda (1990)
A common tariff was established in 1992. Conversations were initiated with Mexico. (Group of Three) to establish a free-trade area (see below).	Aggregate GDP: US$91.3 billion Population: 52 million Total foreign trade: US$34.7 billion Intra-regional trade as percentage of total foreign trade: 1.4
Agreements in the energy sector signed. Negotiations under way.	Aggregate GDP: US$305.8 billion Population: 138.2 million Total foreign trade: US$94.4 billion Intra-regional trade as percentage of total foreign trade: 0.8
Maximum tariff to imports from Chile scheduled to be 20% in 1994. Chile's tariff rate remains at 11%. Tariffs scheduled to reach 0 in 1999.	Aggregate GDP: US$240.2 billion Population: 32.9 million Total foreign trade: US$78.8 billion Intra-regional trade as percentage of total foreign trade: 0.1
Being implemented. In 1992 a partial free-trade agreement with Venezuela was signed that gradually eliminates Venezuelan tariffs.	Aggregate GDP: US$17.1 billion Population: 19.5 million Total foreign trade: US$7.3 billion Intra-regional trade as percentage of total foreign trade: 11.8
Safeguard regime. Technical rules, and dispute resolution agreements under negotiation.	Aggregate GDP: US$240.3 billion Population: 112.4 million Total foreign trade: US$74.2 billion Intra-regional trade as percentage of total foreign trade: 1.6
Agreement signed. Parliamentary ratification still pending.	Aggregate GDP: US$6,204.6 billion Population: 362.7 million Total-foreign trade: US$1,223.8 billion Intra-regional trade as percentage of total foreign trade: 18.8

NOTES

1. For simplicity and deference to Latin American rhetoric, we use the terms economic integration, trade discrimination, and preferential liberalization as if they were interchangeable. Reciprocal trade discrimination (preferences) relevant to the discussion addressed in this paper can be appropriately regarded as a "loose" form of economic integration.

2. Support for the establishment of the European Payments Union (EPU) and the European Coal and Steel Community (ECSC) can also be regarded as a form of U.S. "self-inflicted" discrimination. For a review of the role of discrimination in the international trading system in the early postwar decades, see Patterson (1966).

3. The "structuralist" case in favor of economic integration in Latin America is made in ECLA (1959).

4. For an overview of the process of trade liberalization in Latin America since the mid-1980s, see Bouzas and Lustig (1992).

5. This standard rule needs to be qualified to take into consideration the effect of scale economies, quantitative restrictions, reduced consumption distortions, and trade in intermediate goods. See Wonnacott and Lutz (1989).

6. The classic presentation is in Balassa (1961). See also, El-Agraa (1989).

7. The following citations are useful as a reminder of the skepticism and uncertainty regarding these "gray area dynamic effects," as Bhagwati (1988) calls them:

> Although the arguments for the success of the EP (export-promotion) strategy based on economies of scale and X-efficiency are plausible, empirical support for them is not available. The arguments on savings and innovation provide a less than compelling case for showing that EP is necessarily better on their account than IS (import-substitution). (Bhagwati, 1988, p. 40)

> To date there is no clear cut confirmation of the hypothesis that countries with an external orientation benefit from greater growth in technical efficiency in the components sectors of manufacturing. (Pack, 1990, p. 38)

> If truth in advertising were to apply to policy advice, each prescription for trade liberalization would be accompanied with a disclaimer: "Warning! Trade liberalization cannot be shown to enhance technical efficiency; nor has it been empirically demonstrated to do so." (Rodrik, 1992, p. 172)

The World Bank, although much more assertive on this topic, recognizes that "a degree of skepticism is warranted" (World Bank, 1991, p. 98).

8. For a discussion on how "natural" protection can interact with scale economies to give ambiguous answers as to the strength of the trend towards concentration, see Krugman and Venables (1990). For classic arguments on the operation of "virtuous" and/or "vicious" cycles of accumulation and growth, see Myrdal (1957) and Kaldor (1982).

9. Estimates by Harris and Robertson (1993) are in turn based on the following assumptions: 1) a growth path of per-capita income of 1 percent per year for Canada and the United States; 2) a rate of convergence toward the average per-capita income in the hemisphere similar to the rate at which EEC countries converged after the formation of the Common Market (based on estimates by Ben-David, 1991). The two estimates in the last column represent the results at the lower and upper bound of the standard deviations of Ben-David's estimates. Harris and Robertson then use these estimates to compare with a reference scenario in which Latin American countries converge at the same rate at which the European countries did before the establishment of the Common Market. Since the two convergence rates are very different—the income gap is halved every 13.3 years in one case and every 75 years in the other—the effects of "hemispheric integration" on income convergence are dramatic. As we shall see below, the assumed reference scenario is quite different from the Latin American development experience up to 1980.

10. For an interesting analysis of the issues posed by convergence and divergence in the case of EEC's extension, see Bliss and Braga de Macedo (1990).

11. Given the lack of better alternatives, and along with the usual caveats, reference to the *existing* trade patterns seems unavoidable in assessing these benefits.

12. However, if the starting point is a very distorted trade regime, it is likely that there will still be room to mobilize foreign investment to take full advantage of the opportunities to specialize along the lines of comparative advantage.

13. Scale effects could also arise from rationalization of production structures and reduction of monopolistic pricing practices in import-competing sectors. Yet precisely because of their small market size, these benefits are likely to be reaped as a result of trade liberalization rather than from enlarged market access.

14. As Krugman (1991) points out, in the logic of trade negotiations—or of GATT-think, as he puts it—"1) exports are good; 2) imports

are bad; and 3) other things equal, an equal increase in imports and exports is good." While these principles are unintelligible in the long-run logic of general equilibrium trade theory, they can make a lot of sense in the usually much shorter time horizon of policymakers operating under tight fiscal and balance-of-payments constraints. In practice, countries are likely to be prepared to exchange market access for trade liberalization the larger the net benefits they stand to gain from the former.

15. The fiscal aspects of trade policy reform have also been stressed by a number of authors. See, in particular, Rodrik (1990) and de Melo, Panagariya, and Rodrik (1992). In most Latin American countries, however, fiscal effects are likely to be secondary when compared to the exchange-rate implications of trade liberalization.

16. On the supportive role of the real exchange rate in the process of transition toward a more open trade regime, see Papageorgiou, Machely, and Choksi (1991). Losers from currency depreciation may be more diffused than those negatively affected by trade liberalization in a context of real appreciation of the domestic currency.

17. It is remarkable that in the 1980s, those countries that managed to depreciate domestic currencies substantially and for prolonged periods of time are to be found among those that faced positive fiscal effects from a devaluation (in particular Chile, Colombia, and Mexico). In contrast, traditional exchange-rate dilemmas have become more severe in countries facing a deficit, often substantial, in public foreign-exchange balances (notably Argentina and Brazil). To the extent that trade liberalization raises the exchange rate required to reconcile internal and external balance, it increases—rather than decreases—the required fiscal adjustment. This may go some way into explaining why these stabilization experiences have so far been consistent only with largely overvalued domestic currencies. This can also explain the large degree of real exchange-rate variability in the adjustment process (see Fanelli, Frenkel, and Rozenwurcel, 1990; Ros, 1991).

18. In other words, the "equilibrium" real exchange rate expected by financial markets can differ from what policymakers may regard as appropriate to favor a smooth transition and discourage anti-liberalization coalitions. Krugman (1990) discusses this issue in the context of the EEC's enlargement.

19. See Ros (1993).

20. See, among others, Hart (1990) and Lustig (1992, chapter 5).

21. A CGE model by Brown, Deardorff, and Stern (1992) concludes that with capital mobility ROW's net exports to NAFTA will contract by $11 billion (but ROW's terms of trade will improve 0.2 percent). Another exercise by Sobarzo (1992) concludes that ROW's net exports to Mexico will expand 17 percent.

22. Two frequently mentioned examples are sugar exports for the Caribbean and Central American countries and frozen orange concentrate for Brazil.

23. If the argument is taken beyond reallocation of resources into the realm of market access and dynamic effects, reciprocal trade discrimination between a large and a small partner will imply that the latter will obtain access to a relatively larger market. This may reinforce the reasons for a side payment to bribe the larger country into the agreement. However, as we discussed in Section III, the outcome of a process of economic integration between partners with large differences in income levels is highly uncertain when unfettered market forces allow for the unrestricted operation of polarization effects.

24. In the recent past, the United States was successful in pushing these issues in bilateral and minilateral agreements such as the FTA with Israel, CUSFTA, and NAFTA. It is interesting to note, however, that previous agreements covered less new ground (substantively) than might have originally been expected. CUSFTA, for instance, left out intellectual property rights and grandfathered many existing restrictions on foreign-investment regulations and services. A preliminary assessment attributes a far better record to NAFTA, although some areas were short of some analyst's expectations. See Hufbauer and Schott (1993).

25. Indeed, notwithstanding the convergence, differences in U.S. and Latin American negotiating positions are far from having disappeared completely. In the realm of foreign investment regulation, and although "market" pressures in favor of liberalization are likely to reinforce the overall direction of U.S. policy, individual countries may be inclined to maintain restrictions on a selective basis for national security or other purposes (as Mexico did in the energy sector). In the field of intellectual property rights, monopoly rents and technology transfer issues are also likely to remain controversial. It is also likely that some countries will have a strong preference for maintaining restrictions to foreign trade and investment in various service sectors, particularly in the case of financial, telecommunication, and data-processing activities. Trade in some services of interest to developing countries (like labor services) will also remain an area of divergent negotiating positions.

26. See de Melo, Panagariya, and Rodrik (1992). Moreover, as Bhagwati (1989) points out, taking the labor or social standards issue far enough could suffice to question the very notion of comparative advantage. It is interesting to recall that the "social dumping" case was assiduously raised in the 1950s in regard to Japan's accession to the GATT. See Patterson (1966).

27. The larger efficiency gains become themselves more uncertain when imperfect competition, scale economies, and capital flows are

brought into the picture. The same may or may not be true, however, of dislocation costs, so that the risk of adverse polarization effects tends to fall as market size increases.

28. For a political economy analysis of the contribution of discrimination to trade liberalization, see Oye (1992).

29. This argument is applied to the case of Mexican-U.S. negotiations in Ros (1992).

30. It is likely that the most straightforward way of dealing with this problem is through nonreciprocal liberalization. In the EEC these effects have been tackled by the establishment of adjustment funds.

REFERENCES

Balassa, B. 1961. *The Theory of Economic Integration*. Homewood, Ill.: Irwin.

Baldwin, R. E. 1988. *Trade Policy in a Changing World Economy*. Chicago: University of Chicago Press.

Baldwin, R. 1990. "The Growth Effect of EC-92." *Economic Policy*.

Ben-David, D. 1991. "Equalizing Exchange: A Study of the Effects of Trade Liberalization." National Bureau of Economic Research, Working Paper Series no. 3706.

Bhagwati, J. 1988. "Export-Promoting Trade Strategy: Issues and Evidence." *World Bank Research Observer* 3 (January).

Bliss, C., and J. Braga de Macedo. 1990. *Unity with Diversity in the European Economy: The Community's Southern Frontier*. Cambridge: Cambridge University Press.

Bouzas, R., and N. Lustig. 1992. "Apertura Económica, Integración Regional y la Iniciativa para las Américas." FLACSO/Argentina, *Documentos e Informes de Investigación* no. 132 (July): 1–51.

Brown, D. 1992. "The Impact of a North American Free Trade Area: Applied General Equilibrium Models." In *Assessing the Impact of North American Free Trade*, ed. N. Lustig, B. P. Bosworth, and R. Z. Lawrence. Washington, D.C.: Brookings Institution.

Brown, D., A. Deardorff, and R. Stern. 1992. "A North American Free Trade Agreement: Analytical Issues and a Computational Analysis." *World Economy* 15 (January).

Collins, S. 1992. "Comments." In *Assessing the Impact of North American Free Trade*, ed. N. Lustig, B. P. Bosworth, and R. Z. Lawrence. Washington, D.C.: Brookings Institution.

Corden, M. 1974. *Trade Policy and Economic Welfare*. Oxford: Oxford University Press.

de Melo, J., A. Panagariya, and D. Rodrik. 1992. *Regional Integration: An Analytic and Empirical Overview*. Paper prepared for presentation at the World Bank Conference "New Dimensions in Regional Integration," Washington, D.C.

Dixit, A. 1987. "Issues of Strategic Trade Policies for Small Countries." *Scandinavian Journal of Economics.*

Economic Commission for Latin America. 1959. *The Latin American Common Market.* New York: United Nations.

Economic Commission for Latin America and the Caribbean. 1991. *Statistical Yearbook for Latin America and the Caribbean.* Santiago de Chile: United Nations.

El-Agraa, Ali M. 1989. *The Theory and Measurement of International Economic Integration.* New York: St. Martin's Press.

Erzan, R., and A. Yeats. 1992. "U.S.-Latin American Free Trade Areas: Some Empirical Evidence." In *The Promise and the Premise: Free Trade in the Americas,* ed. S. Saborio et al. New Brunswick: Transaction Books.

Fanelli, J. F., R. Frenkel, and G. Rozenwurcel. 1990. *Growth and Structural Reform in Latin America: Where We Stand.* Buenos Aires: CEDES.

Harris, R. G. 1985. "Summary of a Project on the General Equilibrium Evaluation of Canadian Trade Policy." In *Canada-United States Free Trade,* ed. J. Whalley and R. Hill. Toronto: University of Toronto Press.

Harris, R. G., and P. Robertson. 1993. *Free Trade in the Americas: Estimates on the Economic Impact of a Western Hemispheric Free Trade Area.* Paper prepared for the IDB-ECLAC project on Hemispheric Trade Liberalization.

Hart, M. 1990. *A North American Free Trade Agreement: The Strategic Implication for Canada.* Ottawa: Institute for Research in Public Policy.

Hufbauer, G. C., and J. Schott. 1993. *NAFTA: An Assessment.* Washington, D.C.: Institute for International Economics.

Kaldor, N. 1982. "The Irrelevance of Equilibrium Economics." *Economic Journal* 82: 1237–1255.

Krugman, P. 1990. "Macroeconomic Adjustment and Entry into the EC: A Note." In *Unity with Diversity in the European Economy: The Community's Southern Frontier,* ed. C. Bliss and J. Braga de Macedo. Cambridge: Cambridge University Press.

Krugman, P. 1991. "The Move towards Free Trade Zones." *Federal Reserve Bank of Kansas City Economic Review* (November-December).

Krugman, P., and A. J. Venables. 1992. "Integration and Competitiveness of Peripheral Industry." In *Unity with Diversity in the European Economy: The Community's Southern Frontier,* ed. C.

Bliss and J. Braga de Macedo. Cambridge: Cambridge University Press.

Lee, N. 1992. "Market Structure and Trade in Developing Countries." In *Trade Policy, Industrialization, and Development: New Perspectives*, ed. G. Helleiner. Oxford: Clarendon Press.

Lustig, N. 1992. *Mexico: The Remaking of an Economy*. Washington, D.C.: Brookings Institution.

Mace, G. 1988. "Regional Integration in Latin America: A Long and Winding Road." *International Journal* 43, no. 3 (summer): 404–427.

Myrdal, G. 1957. *Economic Theory and Under-developed Regions*. London: G. Duckworth.

Oye, K. 1992. *Economic Discrimination and Political Change*. Princeton, N.J.: Princeton University Press.

Pack, H. 1990. "Industrialization and Trade." In *Handbook of Development Economics*, ed. H. Chenery and T. N. Srinivasan. New York: North-Holland.

Patterson, G. 1966. *Discrimination in International Trade: The Policy Issues, 1945–1956*. Princeton, N.J.: Princeton University Press.

Papageorgiou, D., M. Machely, and A. Choksi. 1991. *Liberalizing Foreign Trade: Lessons of Experience in the Developing World*. Cambridge, Mass.: Basil Blackwell.

Primo Braga, C. A. 1992. "NAFTA and the Rest of the World." In *Assessing the Impact of North American Free Trade*, ed. N. Lustig, B. P. Bosworth, and R. Z. Lawrence. Washington, D.C.: Brookings Institution.

Richardson, J. David. 1991. "U.S. Trade Policy in the 1980s: Turns—and Roads Not Taken." National Bureau of Economic Research, Working Paper Series no. 3725.

Rodrik, D. 1990. "How Should Structural Adjustment Programs Be Designed?" *World Development* 18, no. 7 (July).

Rodrik, D. 1992. "Closing the Productivity Gap: Does Trade Liberalization Really Help?" In *Trade Policy, Industrialization, and Development: New Perspectives*, ed. G. K. Helleiner. Oxford: Clarendon Press.

Ros, J. 1991. "Domestic Macroeconomic Instability and Integration in the World Economy: Latin America in the 1980s and Prospects for the 1990s." Paper presented at the Inter-American Dialogue workshop on "Latin American Integration in the World Economy: Confronting the Choices," December.

Ros, J. 1992. "Free Trade Area or Common Capital Market? Notes of Mexico-U.S. Economic Integration and Current NAFTA Negotiations." *Journal of Interamerican Studies and World Affairs* 34, no. 2, (summer).

Schott, J. 1989. "More Free Trade Areas?" In *Free Trade Areas and U.S. Trade Policy,* ed. J. Schott. Washington, D.C.: Institute for International Economics.

Sobarzo, H. E. 1992. "A General Equilibrium Analysis of the Gains from Trade for the Mexican Economy of a North American Free Trade Agreement." *World Economy* 15 (January).

Stewart, F., and E. Ghani. 1992. "Externalities, Development, and Trade." In *Trade Policy, Industrialization, and Development: New Perspectives,* ed. G. K. Helleiner. Oxford: Clarendon Press.

Tussie, D. 1987. *The Less Developed Countries and the World Trading System: A Challenge to the GATT.* New York: St. Martin's Press.

Tybout, J. 1992. "Linking Trade and Productivity: New Research Directions." *World Bank Economic Review* 6, no. 2 (May).

Vernon, R., and D. Spar. 1989. *Beyond Globalism.* New York: Free Press.

Weintraub, S. 1984. *Free Trade between Mexico and the United States?* Washington, D.C.: Brookings Institution.

Weintraub, S. 1992. "Modeling the Industrial Effects of NAFTA." In *Assessing the Impact of North American Free Trade,* ed. N. Lustig, B. P. Bosworth, and R. Z. Lawrence. Washington, D.C.: Brookings Institution.

Wonnacott, P., and M. Lutz. 1989. "Is There a Case for Free Trade Areas?" In *Free Trade Areas and U.S. Trade Policy,* ed. J. Schott. Washington, D.C.: Institute for International Economics.

World Bank. 1991. *World Development Report 1991.* Oxford: Oxford University Press.

NAFTA:
Potential Impact on Mexico's Economy and Beyond

Nora Lustig

A NOTE TO THE READER

At the time this paper was written, the negotiations of the North American Free Trade Agreement (NAFTA) had been completed and the agreement had been signed by the executive branches of Canada, Mexico, and the United States. Although the text of the agreement contemplates January 1, 1994, as the starting date of NAFTA, the agreement awaits ratification by the legislative bodies of Mexico and the United States. The Canadian Parliament approved the agreement on June 23, 1993. In addition, at the time this paper was written, the three governments still had to conclude the so-called supplemental agreements on environmental and labor standards first proposed by the new U.S. administration.

The paper's main objective is to present an assessment of the potential impact of NAFTA on the Mexican economy as anticipated, in particular, by the existing empirical analysis. In the final section of the paper, the question of the role of NAFTA as a building block toward hemispheric free trade is addressed. The paper does not discuss the specific content of NAFTA,[1] nor does it address the issue of whether NAFTA will be ratified.

The paper is organized as follows. Section I gives a historical background on Mexico's decision to pursue freer trade with its northern neighbors. Section II describes the trading patterns and barriers among the three countries predating NAFTA. Section III presents an analysis of NAFTA's potential impact on the Mexican economy. Finally, Section IV discusses the role of NAFTA in the process of hemispheric economic integration.

46

I. NAFTA: A Brief Historical Background

A. *Mexico's Metamorphosis: From Import Substitution to the Open-Economy Model*

In the 1980s Mexico made a fundamental shift in its economic strategy.[2] This shift implied a departure from the import-substituting policies of the past, including changes in trade, foreign investment, and exchange-rate regimes, as well as a number of institutional initiatives directed toward expanding and redefining Mexico's role in the world economy. The most salient of the latter include Mexico's joining the General Agreement on Trade and Tariffs (GATT) in 1986 and the negotiation of a free-trade agreement (FTA) with Canada and the United States, completed in 1992.

Industrialization in Mexico in the post–World War II period proceeded under a combination of tariff and non-tariff barriers that protected local production from foreign competition. After 1955, the tariff structure changed little, but protection increased as the number of products subject to import permits or licenses grew. In 1956, 28 percent of the value of imports required permits; by 1970 this had increased to 68 percent. During the balance-of-payments crisis in 1976, they rose to 91 percent. In 1979, in an attempt to liberalize, they fell to 60 percent. Briefly afterwards, this was interrupted as the balance of trade began to deteriorate quickly. In the 1982 balance-of-payments crisis, import permits were reinstated on virtually all products.

The industries subject to protection changed over time. In the 1960s and 1970s, protection favored the production of consumer durables and capital goods, as opposed to consumer non-durables, raw materials, and intermediate goods. In addition to licensing mechanisms, the government relied on domestic content requirements and other policies to stimulate domestic production.[3] Agriculture was the big loser in this policy scheme. It faced substantially lower levels of effective protection; in some years and for some products, it was negative.

To improve the balance of trade in the early 1970s, the government sought to promote exports through selective policy-making, such as tax and tariff rebates, the creation of new institutions in charge of credit provision, and increased promotion of export activities.[4] Later, new sector-specific programs—such as the 1977 program for automobiles and the 1981 program for microcomputers—provided import protection and fiscal incentives in return for export achievements. At the same time, compliance with certain foreign exchange industry-specific balance replaced domestic content requirements.[5]

There is no full assessment of the cost benefits of protectionism in Mexico. Could Mexico have developed an industrial sector without resorting to protectionist practices? Probably not. Was protectionism implemented with "efficiency"? Again, probably not. Industrial output increased steadily during the postwar period. From 1960–1970, the average growth rates of manufacturing were 8.1 percent; they were 6.3 percent from 1970–1980.[6] However, studies available on sources of productivity suggest that the prevailing pattern of growth was extensive; i.e., the result of the factor growth rather than productivity increases.[7]

The 1976 and 1982 balance-of-payments crises made evident that the extensive growth pattern needed to change. If the goal was to raise consumption per capita and reduce the reliance on foreign savings, it was crucial to switch from an extensive growth pattern to one with a rising productivity of investment. Second, the 1982 crisis, in particular, made evident that the capacity of the economy to recover from an external shock depended on the diversity of its sources of foreign revenues and the speed of adjustment of its productive structure in response to changing incentives. Exports and output had to respond more quickly to changes in relative prices. The slower the response, the more negative the impact on output in the face of an adverse external shock. If domestic production could not replace the so-called noncompetitive imports, gross domestic product (GDP) growth rates would have to slow. Third, given the constraints on access to external credit, new sources of capital, such as foreign investment and official bilateral and multilateral credit, had to be attracted. Finally, because of the macroeconomic restrictions, the government could not jump-start the economy through expansionary fiscal policies without putting stabilization at stake. The private sector had to be enticed to lead the recovery by introducing confidence-building measures and opening new investment opportunities.

These four considerations were the basis for the outward-oriented reforms that began in mid-1985. The reforms affected primarily the prevailing trade and foreign investment regimes. Trade liberalization, relaxed restrictions, and institutional initiatives such as the decision to join GATT on foreign ownership, adapting Mexican legislation to international standards, have been the essential ingredients of the new policymaking. Institutional initiatives such as the decision to join GATT also have been part of the strategy.

B. Seeking Closer Ties with the United States: From Piecemeal Agreements to NAFTA

The decision to pursue an FTA with the United States announced in 1990 was congruent with the new development strategy. However, it was an initiative of quite a different nature from the others. An FTA had never been part of the structural reform menu advocated by the multilateral financial institutions. It also marked a radical departure from the previous historical character of the Mexico–United States relationship. The decision to pursue such an FTA was probably prompted by the Mexican government's recognition that in order to translate adjustment into growth, an additional big institutional push was needed. Reduced wages, abundant reforms, and a Brady-type debt accord did not produce the expected economic turnaround quickly enough. The presumption was that an FTA could simultaneously open up new investment opportunities and improve the expected returns from such an investment by reducing the uncertainty in connection with market access and the trends in Mexico's domestic policy.

In March 1990 it was learned that Mexican officials were exploring the idea of an FTA with their U.S. counterparts.[8] This triggered a lot of activity in both administrations to prepare for the subsequent formalities. Later in the year, President Salinas made a formal request to start talks on an agreement. In September 1990, President Bush responded by notifying Congress that he would like to pursue negotiations. The following February, President Bush announced that the negotiations would include Canada.[9] In late May 1991, after several months of often bitter debate between those in favor and those opposed to "fast-track" procedures and/or an FTA with Mexico, the U.S. Congress approved the extension of "fast-track" procedures for two more years beginning June 1991.[10] Negotiations were concluded on August 12, 1992,

and the North American Free Trade Agreement (NAFTA) was
signed by the three executive branches on December 17 of the
same year. If NAFTA is approved by the three legislatures, it
should come into effect on January 1, 1994.

Only a few years ago, a proponent of an FTA between
Mexico and the United States would have faced harsh criticism
in Mexico, and indifference in the United States.[11] For decades in
Mexico, the idea of explicitly promoting increased commercial ties
with the United States and taking part in a bargaining process with
the "imperial power" to the north was blatantly rejected in most
political and academic circles. Officials in the United States,
acknowledging Mexico's feelings of distrust, probably did not
consider an FTA possible, nor did they consider it necessarily a
desirable goal, since multilateralism was the accepted trade strategy in the United States during the post–World War II period.[12]
Bilateral initiatives tended to be viewed as a diversion of institutional efforts, and counterproductive to the overall strategy.

The news of Mexico's intentions initially came as quite a
surprise. However, for the close observer it is apparent that the
Mexican government's attitude toward the United States had become increasingly more cooperative and pragmatic since 1983.
Signing an FTA with the United States was, to a large extent, a
natural evolution of a process that began in Mexico some time
after the eruption of the debt crisis in mid-1982.

As mentioned above, from 1985 to 1989 Mexico vastly
reduced the use of import licenses and harmonized tariffs by
reducing their average and maximum levels (Tables 2.1 and 2.2).
In the period between 1982 and 1989, Mexico's maximum tariff
fell from 100 percent to 20 percent, while the production-weighted
average tariff fell from 23.5 percent to 12.8 percent. Also, by
the end of 1987, the government had eliminated "import official
reference prices," which had been used in some sectors to bypass
liberalization.[13]

The Mexican government also undertook a series of bilateral
efforts designed to improve trade relations with the United States.
Between 1985 and 1989 Mexico and the United States signed a
number of significant agreements.[14] In mid-1985 both countries
signed the Bilateral Understanding on Subsidies and Countervailing Duties. This agreement gave Mexico access to procedures that
included a "material" injury test. In November 1987, it signed the

Table 2.1
Import Trade Liberalization Schedule in Mexico, Main Events and Characteristics, 1983–89

		First Stage		Second Stage		Third Stage
Concept	Financial crisis import restrictions (situation in Dec. 1982)	Gradual opening (Jan. 1, 1983, to July 24, 1985)	July 1985 reform (July 25, 1985, to Dec. 31, 1985)	Deepening of reform and entrance to GATT (Jan. 1, 1986, to Dec. 14, 1987)	Economic Solidarity Pact (Dec. 15, 1987, to Dec. 31, 1988)	Stability and Economic Growth Pact (Jan. 1989 to March 15, 1989)
Import license requirements	100% of imports brought under license requirements	Gradual liberalization begins, extended to 16.4% of imports by Dec. 1984[a]	July 25, 1985, decree: liberalization extended to 64.1% of imports	Liberalization extended to 73.2% of imports	Liberalization extended gradually to 78.2% of imports[b]	— —
Import tariffs	Dec. 31, 1982 Mean: 27.0% Levels: 16 Range: 0–100%	Simplification of tariff schedule (June 30, 1985) Mean: 21.8% Levels: 10 Range: 0–100%	July 25, 1985, decree: tariff increases to compensate reduction of license requirements (Dec. 31, 1985) Mean: 25.2% Levels: 10 Range: 0–100%	April 30, 1986, and March 6, 1987 decrees: GATT tariff reductions (Dec. 4, 1987) Mean: 19.0% Levels: 7 Range: 0–40%	Dec. 15, 1987 decree: Economic Solidarity Pact tariff reductions Mean: 10.4% Levels: 5 Range: 0–20%	Jan. 11, 1989 and March 9, 1989 decrees: tariff increases to diminish dispersion (March 10, 1989) Mean: 10.1% Levels: 5 Range: 0–20%
Import official reference prices (ORPs)	— —	ORPs extended to 4.7% of imports[c]	ORPs for 9.1% of imports	ORPs virtually eliminated. Reduced to 0.5% of imports[d]	Jan. 11, 1988, ORPs eliminated	

Source: USITC, *Review of Trade and Investment Liberalization Measures*, Phase I, Table 4–1, p. 4–2.

[a] This gradual liberalization process continued throughout the first half of 1985 (711 more items liberalized). The aim was to extend freedom from license requirement to 35–45 percent of total imports by December 1995. The July 25, 1985 decree, however, abruptly changed the pace by liberalizing 3,064 items out of a total 8,068 tariff items.

[b] Calculations made with import/export data for the period July–November 1988 using the Harmonized Tariff System.

[c] Data for Dec. 31, 1984. There were no changes in ORPs from this date until April 1985.

[d] Data for Dec. 15, 1987. The figure is representative for Dec. 15, 1987, because ORPs did not change between those dates. Most of the dismantling of ORPs (from 960 to 53 items) occurred between March and July 1987.

Table 2.2
Measures of Trade Liberalization, 1985–1990
(In percent)

	1985	1986	1987	1988	1989	1990
Domestic Production Covered by Import Licenses	92.2	46.9	35.8	23.2	22.1	19.0
Production-Weighted Tariff Averages	23.5	24.0	22.7	11.0	12.8	12.5
Domestic Production Covered by Official Reference Prices	18.7	19.6	13.4	0.0	0.0	0.0

Note: The information is for June of each year.

Source: Adriaan Ten Kate, *The Mexican Trade Liberalization of 1985–1987*, mimeo (Mexico City), cited by Claudia Schatan in "Trade Bargaining: The Mexican Case," paper presented at SELA Caracas, Venezuela (February 5–7, 1991), Tables 1, 2, and 3.

U.S.-Mexico "Framework of Principles and Procedures for Consultation Regarding Trade and Investment Relations," considered a landmark in bilateral economic relations. This was followed by sectoral accords in the areas of steel and textiles. In 1989, the two countries signed another comprehensive agreement, "Understanding Regarding Trade and Investment Facilitation Talks" (TIFTs).

In the second half of the 1980s, both countries had acquired substantial experience and knowledge about each other's trade practices, institutional characteristics, and bargaining procedures. This experience constituted a solid basis for making the negotiations of a free-trade agreement possible. As one author has put it, "a[n] important byproduct of the substantial trade liberalization implemented by the De la Madrid administration since July 1985 has been the reduction or elimination of numerous long-standing bilateral trade irritants."[15]

An example of increased goodwill in trade-related bilateral relations was the evolution of Mexico's eligibility to benefit from the General System of Preferences. In 1987 a number of products were removed from the list to show dissatisfaction with changes made to Mexico's intellectual property laws.[16] In 1989, of the

306 products that Mexico wished to reincorporate, 275 were approved.[17]

Besides the trade matters, there have been other areas of bilateral economic cooperation that underscore the change in U.S.-Mexican relations. These include the implementation of the U.S. bilateral cooperative program in agriculture; joint agreements on investment and tourism promotion; agreements on environmental problems; agreements on management of television signals and radio spectra along the border; agreements on the exchange of tax information; and the negotiation of a bilateral income-tax treaty.[18]

The Mexican government had also approached Canada in a move to intensify its trade and investment relations. In March 1990 both countries signed the Canada-Mexico Framework Agreement on bilateral trade and economic relations. Though it was not clear whether Mexico was ready to "include" Canada in its FTA agenda, it clearly wanted to leave the door open for such an alternative or, at the least, not to make the Canadians feel left out of the process.

C. Why an FTA?

Early in the Salinas Administration, it seemed that the emphasis of his government would be placed on a "plurilateral" approach. The objective of the approach would be to increase trade and attract investment from the world at large. The relationship with the United States would continue to be promoted through sectoral accords to the extent that these were possible. The decision to seek an FTA with the United States did not contradict the previous strategy of the Mexican government in any fundamental way. However, it signaled an important shift in the emphasis given to formal bonds with the United States. What explains this shift?

When foreign investment did not respond with the expected vigor to the Brady-type debt agreement (in principle) signed in mid-1989, and its far-reaching economic reforms, the Mexican government had to find new ways to entice the capital inflows required for economic recovery and sustained growth.[19] Policies able to increase the expected rate of return on investment and boost private-sector confidence were of the essence. A free-trade agreement with the United States belonged to this category for two reasons in particular. An FTA would ensure: a) future access to the U.S. market, and b) the durability of Mexico's open economy strategy.[20] The fears and uncertainties produced by the failure of the Uruguay Round of GATT and the "fortress" Europe of 1992 may have influenced the decision to seek an FTA with the United States.

The decision did not prevent the Mexican government from continuing to act on its plurilateral approach. It did not abandon multilateral action and pursued other bilateral initiatives. Mexico was active in the· Uruguay Round and joined the Pacific Basin Agreement. Mexico also signed a free-trade agreement with Chile in 1991 and committed itself to seeking free-trade agreements with Central America,[21] and with Colombia and Venezuela.[22] At the same time, Mexico assiduously pursued strengthened ties with Europe and Japan.[23]

II. THE STARTING POINT: TRADE FLOWS AND TRADE BARRIERS

In 1989 trade between Mexico and the United States equaled US$52 billion.[24] Almost 70 percent of Mexico's exports go to the United States and about the same proportion of its imports come from the United States (Table 2.3). In contrast, trade with Mexico has recently represented between 5 to 6 percent of total U.S. imports.[25] These figures illustrate the serious asymmetry in the bilateral relationship between Mexico and the United States—as there is between Canada and the United States. Given the relative weight of the United States as a source of imports and a market for exports, the bilateral liberalization for Mexico, strictly speaking, means liberalization in full.

Trade between Mexico and Canada is comparatively modest. In 1989 it reached C$2.3 billion, accounting for 1.2 percent of Mexico's total exports and 1.8 percent of its total imports (Table 2.3). In 1989 Mexico's share in Canada's imports equaled 1.3 percent, and 0.5 percent in Canada's exports. Although Canadian imports from Mexico are not extensive, they have been growing rapidly; in 1989 they increased by 27.9 percent.[26]

Table 2.3
Mexico's Major Trading Partners
(In percent)

Countries	1989 Exports	1989 Imports	1990 Exports	1990 Imports
Total	100.0	100.0	100.0	100.0
Western Hemisphere	78.5	73.9	77.9	71.4
United States	69.3	68.0	69.7	64.6
Canada	1.2	1.8	0.9	1.5
Latin-American Integration Association[a]	3.3	3.0	3.2	4.1
Argentina	0.5	0.6	0.4	1.3
Brazil	0.9	1.5	0.6	1.4
Venezuela	0.3	0.2	0.5	0.6
Others	1.7	0.6	1.7	0.8
Central American Common Market[b]	1.9	0.4	1.6	0.3
Others	2.8	1.0	2.5	0.9
Western Europe	12.5	16.9	13.6	18.4
European Economic Community[c]	11.4	14.3	12.7	15.6
European Free Trade Association[d]	0.8	2.6	0.9	2.6
Others	0.3	0.0	0.0	0.2
Asia	8.4	7.4	7.9	8.6
Japan	5.8	4.5	5.6	4.7
Others	2.6	2.8	2.3	3.9
Rest of the World	0.6	1.8	0.6	1.6
Eastern Europe	0.1	0.3	0.1	0.4
Others	0.5	1.5	0.5	1.2

Source: Banco de México, *The Mexican Economy: 1991* (Mexico City: 1991), 223.

[a]The Latin American Integration Association comprises Argentina, Brazil, Bolivia, Colombia, Chile, Ecuador, Paraguay, Peru, Uruguay, and Venezuela.
[b]The Central American Common Market comprises Costa Rica, El Salvador, Guatemala, Honduras, and Nicaragua.
[c]The European Economic Community comprises West Germany, Belgium-Luxembourg, France, Italy, The Netherlands, United Kingdom, Denmark, Ireland, Greece, Spain, and Portugal.
[d]The European Free Trade Association comprises Austria, Finland, Norway, Sweden, Switzerland, and Iceland.

It is evident, then, that the bilateral relationship between Canada and Mexico cannot be the sole motivation for seeking free trade between them. Both want to have free trade with the United States, and Canada wants to avoid the trade or investment diversion effects that would result from not sharing in the benefits granted to Mexico in a bilateral agreement.

Trade between Mexico and the United States is relatively free. It is certainly much freer than it was before Mexico's trade liberalization and the sectoral agreements signed between both countries. According to the estimates of the Mexican Secretariat of Commerce and Industrial Promotion, the average trade-weighted tariff on Mexican imports from the United States was about 11 percent in May 1988 and 12.6 percent in March 1989, whereas Mexican exports faced an average imported-weighted tariff of between 3 and 6 percent in the United States.[27] More than 80 percent of Mexican exports enter the United States in the duty range of 0 to 5 percent, with about 26 percent entering duty-free, either under the GSP[28] or at reduced effective rates under the *maquiladora* program. Similarly, under the same program a share of U.S. exports to Mexico enter duty free if they are reexported.[29]

However, many Mexican products faced a U.S. tariff higher than the 20 percent maximum tariff prevailing in Mexico.[30] Clearly, there was room for trade creation through further reductions on both sides. Nonetheless, the elimination of non-tariff barriers was probably more important to both countries. For example, about 20 percent of imports into Mexico (before NAFTA) were still subject to licensing, with import licenses for agricultural products and livestock the most widespread.[31] The automotive sector was still subject to important restrictions. The United States also placed important restrictions on the import of textiles, steel, and agricultural products.[32]

In the United States, protectionism often creeps in, disguised through what is called "contingent protectionism." This occurs when U.S. producers, faced with alleged unfair trade practices, such as foreign subsidies or "dumping," take or threaten to take action to limit trade or impose countervailing duties.[33] In practice, charges of unfairness presented by U.S. producers have become a common protective device. This is one kind of protectionism that the Mexican government—like its Canadian counterpart—is particularly keen on eliminating.

Canadian imports from Mexico face low barriers even before NAFTA is put in place. In fact, 82 percent of Mexican exports to Canada entered duty-free in 1989, either under the most-favored-nation principle or the Canadian General Preference treatment. Higher duties prevailed in labor-intensive sectors such as textiles and clothing.[34] Many Canadian and Mexican manufacturers compete directly in certain segments of the United States and other markets. Mexico's labor-cost advantage has thus prompted fear in Canada that as the remaining tariff barriers disappear, Canadian workers will suffer. The risks of labor displacement, however, should not be exaggerated, because several factors, such as lower productivity and poorer infrastructure, offset Mexico's labor-cost advantage.[35]

III. NAFTA's Potential Impact on the Mexican Economy

Is NAFTA going to contribute toward improved living conditions and a modernized economy in Mexico? As we shall see in this section, the results obtained from available applied research consistently show that the elimination of tariff and non-tariff barriers among Canada, Mexico, and the United States will have a positive effect on Mexican real incomes.

In addition, existing modeling exercises do not fully capture other factors that increase the positive contribution of NAFTA to Mexico's modernization. For one thing, there is no precise estimate of the confidence-enhancing effect on investment flows derived from the decline in uncertainty, in terms both of Mexico's staying on course with its open-economy policies and of reducing United States' use of contingent protectionism. Second, greater integration could have a positive impact on productivity well beyond that generated by a more efficient allocation of resources, because of a more rapid introduction of modern technologies in the production and management processes, and a more rapid closing of what has been called the "idea gap."[36]

A. NAFTA's Impact on Mexico: What the Available Economic Models Tell You

Soon after learning that Mexico and the United States were exploring the possibility of signing a free trade agreement, scholars in both countries began to work on estimating the potential impact of such an agreement on both economies. Not long afterward the research incorporated Canada, even before it was made official that it would participate in the negotiations giving rise to NAFTA. At the outset, one should say that all the empirical analysis "predicts" a much larger relative impact for Mexico than for Canada or the United States. This should come as no surprise, because the Mexican economy is so much smaller than the other two, particularly that of the United States (Table 2.4).

Among economists, the preferred vehicle to estimate the potential impact of a change in trade policy is the so-called computable general equilibrium model (CGE).[37] The reason behind this preference is that CGEs provide a consistent framework designed to capture the adjustment and interaction of product and factor markets to changes in exogenous policy variables such as tariffs and non-tariff barriers (NTBs). According to Brown, CGEs "attempt to bring together the theoretical understanding of market behavior with key features of the economies involved."[38] CGEs are particularly useful because they provide results at the sectoral level, as well as for distributive variables such as real wages (or employment, depending on the assumptions) and the rate of return on capital, within a framework that ensures aggregate consistency and incorporates supply constraints.

In the last ten years the technology that surrounds the building of CGEs has become increasingly sophisticated. Initially CGEs generally did not go beyond the all-too-idealistic assumption of perfect competition and constant returns to scale.[39] At present, there are many variants of CGEs that assume increasing returns to scale and imperfect competition, with imperfect competition modeled making alternative assumptions about the behavior of price-setting agents. We see models that attempt to incorporate dynamic mechanisms and the market for financial assets. In addition, the models have increasingly incorporated relationships designed to better capture the specificities of the countries involved—for example, rural-urban migration. Finally, we see an increasing use of CGE techniques applied to multi-country interactions (e.g., migration flows and capital flows).

In the particular case of NAFTA, economists have used many CGEs featuring various assumptions.[40] The main characteristics of the models are summarized in the Appendix, and the results in

Table 2.4
Relative Size of the Canadian, Mexican,
and U.S. Economies, 1990

	Canada	Mexico	United States
GDP (billions of US dollars)	572	214	55,214
Population (millions)	26.6	86.1	250.0
Per capita GDP (US dollars)	21,527	2,490	22,055
Average wage per day (US dollars)	67.98[a]	8.11[b]	69.14[c]

Sources: Comisión Nacional de los Salarios Mínimos; World Bank, *World Development Report, 1992* (Washington, 1992); Statistics Canada; *Economic Report of the President, January 1992*; and Department of Commerce, Bureau of Economic Analysis.

[a]Based on average weekly earnings of employees paid by the hour.
[b]Average daily wages in the formal sector (covered by social security).
[c]Based on average weekly earnings for nonsupervisory workers in private nonagricultural industries.

terms of NAFTA's impact on Mexican wages, income, and employment are presented in Table 2.5. An examination of the results yields the following conclusions:

1. The overall potential *direct* impact of NAFTA on Mexico's real income is positive but small. The estimates range from the order of one-third of one percentage point to over three percent, depending on the assumptions about technology and market structure, and whether the model is static or dynamic. These aspects are further discussed below.

2. The removal of NTBs has greater potential impact on real income than the removal of tariffs: see the results for the Roland-Holst, Reinert, and Shiells I, and Trela and Whalley models. The order of magnitude will depend on the modeling assumptions, as discussed below.

3. The *indirect* impact of NAFTA on real income measured, for example, by the rise in capital inflows induced by NAFTA, is more significant (between three to twenty times larger depending on the model) than the impact of eliminating tariffs and NTBs. The results show an increase in Mexico's real income that ranges from 4 to 8 percent. Employment also rises by many multiples when capital inflows are assumed to happen.

Table 2.5
NAFTA's Impact on Mexican Wages, Employment,
and Income: Modeling Results
(Percent change)

Computable General Equilibrium	Wage[a]	Employment	Rent	Real Income
Static and CRS[c]				
KPMG Peat Marwick				
Tariffs and NTBs	—	0.85	0.60	0.32
Tariffs, NTBs and K-Inflow	—	6.60	0.0	4.64
Hinojosa and Robinson				
Tariffs and NTBs	R: -0.2	—	1.1	0.3
	US: -0.2	—		
	S: 1.0	—		
	WC: 1.0	—		
Tariffs, NTBs and K-Inflow[b]	R: -9.2	—	-1.2	6.4
	US: 9.2	—		
	S: 7.4	—		
	WC: 8.8	—		
Tariffs, NTBs, K-Inflow, and endogenous migration	R: 4.7	—	-0.9	6.8
	US: 4.7	—		
	S: 7.7	—		
	WC: 9.1	—		
Roland-Holst, Reinert, and Shiells I				
Tariffs	—	0.33	0.45	0.11
Tariffs and NTBs	—	1.49	5.18	2.28
Trela and Whalley				
Textiles	—	—	—	1.2
Steel	—	—	—	1.6
Static and IRS				
Roland-Holst, Reinert, and Shiells II				
Cournot Solution	—	1.73	5.77	2.47
Contestable Solution	—	2.40	6.57	3.29

Table 2.5 *continued*

Computable General Equilibrium	Wage[a]	Employment	Rent	Real Income
Sobarzo				
Exogenous Wage and sectorally fixed capital stocks	–	5.1	6.2	2.0
Exogenous and inter-sectorally employment mobile capital	16.2	–	0.0	2.2
Brown, Deardorrf, and Stern				
Tariffs and NTBs	0.7	–	0.6	1.6
Tariffs, NTBs and K-inflows	9.3	–	3.3	5.0
Dynamic Models				
Young and Romero				
Complete Liberalization (gain over base steady state)	–	–	–	2.6
Liberalization and interest rate reduced from 10% to 7.67% (gain over base steady state)	–	–	–	8.1
Levy & Van Wijnbergen				
Maize Liberalization Total	–	–	–	0.6
Subsistence Farmers	–	–	–	-3.3
Landless rural workers	–	–	–	-1.6
Rainfed farmers	–	–	–	-5.7
Irrigated farmers	–	–	–	2.8
Urban workers	–	–	–	1.6
Urban capitalists	–	–	–	1.8

Source: Drusilla Brown, "The Impact of a North American Free Trade Area: Applied General Equilibrium Models," *North American Free Trade: Assessing the Impact*, Brookings Institution, 1992, Table 2 (p. 36), Table 5 (p. 47), Table 8 (p. 54) and Raúl Hinojosa-Ojeda and Sherman Robinson, "Labor Issues in a North American Free Trade," in *North American Free Trade: Assessing the Impact*, Brookings Institution, 1992, p. 79.

[a]R: rural workers; US: urban unskilled worker; S: skilled worker; WC: white collar.
[b]Exogenous capital inflow identical to Peat Marwick study.
[c]CRS: constant returns to scale; IRS: increasing returns to scale.

4. In the absence of capital inflows, the distributive impact could be "regressive" (i.e., rural workers, small peasants and unskilled workers could lose) *if agriculture (maize in particular) is liberalized*. However, if capital inflows and productivity gains are accounted for, the poorest segments of the population have the most to gain from NAFTA.

The results of the simulations are sensitive to the assumptions made in the models. In particular, there are three kinds of assumptions which can have a quantitatively significant impact:

i) *National product differentiation*. With the exception of that used by Trela and Whalley, all of the models assume that products are differentiated by geographic origin (e.g., domestic versus imported). This assumption (known as the Armington assumption) implies that consumers differentiate goods by place of production.[41] It has been found that product differentiation on both the import and the export sides tends to dampen the response of domestic prices to fluctuations in export and import prices. Essentially, fluctuations in the latter are imperfectly transmitted to the domestic price system and, thus, the impact of these fluctuations (induced by a change in trade policy, for example) on resource allocation and factor prices is much milder. This explains why, in the case of Trela and Whalley's model, the removal of NTBs in just one of the sectors (steel, textiles, or apparel) can have such a large impact on Mexico's real income: the dampening effect is not present.[42]

ii) *Returns to scale and competition*. The first generation of CGEs assumed constant returns to scale (CRS) technology[43] and perfect competition. In these models the observed low degree of specialization in production was captured in the national product differentiation assumption that was previously discussed. The latter, however, is considered to be the wrong way to model the observed low degree of specialization.[44] Several authors have suggested, instead, that the low degree of specialization may result from imperfect competition and the presence of increasing returns to scale (IRS) in technologies.[45] A good illustration of the impact that a change in assuming CRS or IRS may have can be seen in comparing the results presented by the Roland-Holst, Reinert and Shiells model in its two versions (Table 2.5). In their IRS version of the model, the gains in real income are higher;

interestingly, however, what seems to matter the most is the assumption about price-setting behavior of firms in an imperfectly competitive environment.[46]

iii) *"Dynamic" considerations*: The first and second generations of CGEs have been static. These models leave out many important questions. For example, static models are unable to provide estimates of the implications of a free-trade agreement for the trade balance, exchange rates, and capital formation. Dynamic models must try to incorporate intertemporal utility and profit maximization, and attitudes toward risk and uncertainty.[47] Dynamic models indicate a larger impact on real income than static ones for equivalent experiments (e.g., elimination of tariffs only). Compare, for example, the results of Roland-Holst, Reinert, and Shiells I and Young and Romero in Table 2.5.[48] In the former, the potential impact on real income is equal to 0.11 percent, whereas in the latter it is 2.6 percent.

B. Models and the "Real World"

What do we learn from these models and how should their results be used in the "real world"? The orders of magnitude presented in the various experiments should not be taken as actual predictions. The main difficulty stems from the fact that actual outcomes can be significantly affected by unforeseen exogenous events that occur simultaneously with the foreseen policy change.[49] Furthermore as we will see in the following section, the models leave out some very important economic interactions that can affect the actual course of the variables.

Nonetheless, if the results are systematic, they are at least indicative of the direction of the expected change and of the possible ranking obtained from different liberalization scenarios. As such, all models predict that the impact of free trade on Mexico's total real income will be positive; that removing NTBs is at least as important as eliminating tariffs, if not more so; and— *above all*—that factor movements (capital and labor) have a much more important effect on the country's economic performance than do reducing tariffs and eliminating import quotas.

If one would have to choose among the alternative model specifications based on their "realism," the preferred models are those that assume increasing returns to scale, noncompetitive market structures, product differentiation (in particular, by firms), and capital and labor inflows.[50] These put the potential impact of NAFTA on Mexico's real income in the 5 to 8 percent range, equivalent to between two and three years of GDP growth if it were to grow at the annual rate observed for 1989–1992.

Are these exercises useful in guiding policy? Did they play a role in determining the outcome of the actual NAFTA completed on August 12, 1992? The models have probably had more impact on reinforcing the overall positive assessment of NAFTA by the negotiating and participating actors than in guiding the negotiations in any specific way. There may be one exception: the potential impact on employment and migration from a quick liberalization of the corn sector in Mexico found in the simulations may have contributed to the decision to go slow on agriculture.[51] A quick liberalization of the corn sector could have produced a relatively large displacement of labor, with the consequential negative impact on wages of the urban unskilled workers and the incomes of the rural poor. See the results of Levy and Van Wijnbergen's exercise in Table 2.5.[52]

C. *The Potential Impact of NAFTA on Mexico: Beyond the Simulation Models*

The NAFTA is expected to have important effects on Mexico's economic performance that are not captured by the modeling exercises. In particular, two should be emphasized. The first has to do with the confidence-enhancing impact of NAFTA (i.e., the link between NAFTA and policy credibility) and its effect on stimulating capital inflows. At present, large capital inflows represent a crucial ingredient to ensure Mexico's consolidation of low inflation rates and economic restructuring. These inflows bridge the gap between today's need for large amounts of investment and the expected future gains in productivity. Nonetheless, it is fair to say that not everybody is convinced that these inflows will smooth the way for a process that is internally consistent.

Some authors have expressed concern that the capital inflows induced by NAFTA in the short run ratify a macroeconomic program that combines policies not consistent in the long run. In particular, those capital inflows may support a real exchange rate congruent with the inflation goals but not with higher growth rates of Mexico's GDP.[53]

The second NAFTA-related effect has to do with the longer-run impact of economic integration on productivity growth. Piore contends that "models do not predict the very large, discontinuous effects from the opening to trade that are associated with the most spectacular success stories in East Asia."[54] History and economic insight suggest that increasing economic integration will lead to a positive impact on productivity growth associated with technological and organizational innovation and learning. In fact, current growth theory concludes that these factors are paramount in explaining a country's performance.

The actual NAFTA does more than reduce tariffs and remove quantitative restrictions.[55] Non-tariff barriers take other forms in addition to quantitative restrictions, and NAFTA includes rules for intellectual property and investment. It also includes rules for pollution and incorporates provisions for the administration of trade. Moreover, the supplemental agreements on environmental and labor standards will likely set in motion a process of long-run harmonization in the standards and trigger an improvement in the enforcement mechanisms in Mexico. While many aspects of NAFTA are directed toward reducing barriers and contingent protectionist practices, thus amplifying the positive effect of free trade in the narrowest sense, other aspects such as the tendencies to harmonize environmental and worker safety standards set in motion by NAFTA may actually increase costs and dampen part of the liberalizing effects.[56]

Finally, it is not only the benefits but also the costs—in particular, those associated with the transitional period—that may be underestimated by the existing assessments. NAFTA may have at least two other important consequences whose order of magnitude is unknown. The "losers" and "winners" of NAFTA-related liberalization will likely be in sectors perceived or defined as homogeneous and, thus, the actual disruption of implementing NAFTA would be greater than anticipated. Also, the speed of liberalization may have a greater impact on the final outcome than one expects. In some sectors the agreed pace of liberalization may eliminate producers who, given more time, could have survived. If the transitional costs are very high (i.e., in terms of displaced labor), a longer phase-out should probably have been preferred. The actual NAFTA has several liberalization schedules ranging from 0 to 15 years. It is not clear to what extent these responded to a calculation of the costs and benefits involved in the transition phase, or to the relative power of the industries pushing in favor of longer or shorter phase-outs.[57]

IV. NAFTA and Hemispheric Integration

A. *Potential Impact of NAFTA on the Rest of Latin America and the Caribbean*

The creation of NAFTA has generated substantial concern in the rest of Latin America and the Caribbean (LAC). The main concern is that NAFTA may shift trade and investment flows away from countries other than Mexico. Clearly the impact of NAFTA on trade and investment flows will vary from country to country. Available estimates of NAFTA's impact on the rest of the hemisphere show that, on average, the effects will be relatively small. For example, Primo Braga indicates that the elimination of tariffs among the three NAFTA countries will cause exports from LAC to the United States to fall by about 0.7 percent.[58] In addition, another study estimates that 94 percent of the trade diversion generated by NAFTA will affect countries outside the region. According to the numbers, this would mean that trade diversion for LAC would be of the order of $28 million.[59]

These estimates, however, may not be very accurate or helpful. First of all, countries that today enjoy preferential treatment in their trade with the United States (e.g., the Caribbean and Central America) fear that in the current policy environment preferences will be phased out. At the same time, the competition for market access to the United States will become tougher because Mexico is a country with similar characteristics, particularly in terms of labor costs. Second, NAFTA may cause investment diversion. Investment diversion could have macroeconomic consequences (since other countries in the region need foreign investment to ensure macroeconomic consistency and growth just as Mexico does) and could affect future trade flows. Finally, the actual agreement may include provisions that are more discriminatory than the *ante* situation for the non-NAFTA countries (in the rules of origin, for example).

B. NAFTA as a Building Block of Hemispheric Free Trade

Ever since it was known that the United States and Mexico were considering a free-trade agreement, other countries in the region started to show their desire to be next in line. In June 1990 the United States manifested its interest in promoting the idea of hemispheric free trade in what became known as the "Enterprise for the Americas Initiative." Most governments in the region welcomed the idea. At some point it seemed that hemispheric free trade became the ultimate goal, both of the process of unilateral liberalization as well as the initiatives of subregional integration. From 1990 onward, one can observe attempts to revamp old arrangements of economic integration (for example, the Central American Common Market [CACM] and the Andean Pact), to accelerate ongoing processes (Mercosur, for example) and to create new ones (for example, the Group of Three, Chile-Mexico, and CACM-Mexico).[60]

As soon as the concept of hemispheric free trade became a possibility, analysts began trying to imagine how this might be accomplished; they recommended certain paths and rejected others.[61] One group of authors, most of them from Canada, have expressed their concern that the process of economic integration in the hemisphere will be of the "hub-and-spoke" variety with the United States at the center. Under such a scenario the United States would become the only country with tariff-free access to the markets of all participating countries. The hub would benefit; the spokes would lose.[62] The spokes may be individual countries, non-overlapping subregional trading arrangements, or even overlapping ones. In turn, the spokes may sign free-trade agreements among themselves, generating a crisscross pattern that, while reducing the trade diversion effects and efficiency losses present in the pure hub-and-spoke case, would be a maze of different rules of origin and dispute-settlement mechanisms. In practice the arrangement could hamper the free flow of goods and services.

The ideal strategy would be to sign a comprehensive free-trade agreement among all the parties involved (individual countries and/or subregional arrangements). From the point of view of economic welfare, administrative simplicity in its operation, and political balance among the participants, there is no doubt that such a course would be the best. However, there is one problem. Such a course is highly unlikely to happen, because it would require an amount of leadership and consensus in the region that neither exists at present nor seems likely in the future.

If a comprehensive arrangement is ruled out, what is the best course? Should NAFTA become the linchpin of hemispheric integration? In principle, NAFTA has the potential to become the core agreement with other countries or subregions joining in. The so-called accession clause included in NAFTA indicates that the agreement is open to new members (from anywhere in the world) as long as the interested party is willing to subscribe to the agreement and the member countries agree.

The problem is that most countries in the region may not view NAFTA as the core agreement. After all, it includes provisions that were custom-made for the current members of NAFTA. On the other hand, individual countries in the region have an incentive to become a spoke of the United States because this would ensure access to the large market, and there may be some "first-come, first-blessed" effect that the traditional assessment of the hub-and-spoke model does not capture. In addition, individual countries or subregions may find it easier to negotiate with one member of NAFTA, particularly the most powerful one, than with all of the members.[63]

An alternative path that may be more feasible in practical terms, is to let the United States take the initiative to negotiate agreements with individual countries and subregions using the subset of NAFTA as the real core. As such a process occurs, it is likely that the other members of NAFTA will want to join in the negotiations for the same reason that Canada wanted to join in when it learned about Mexico and the United States. This process may produce the necessary leadership and generate the tendency for the desirable harmonization implicitly, rather than by a mandate crafted through institutional arrangements that may never get off the ground. The result will not be as "pure" as that which would follow a comprehensive agreement approach. The advantage of the "implicit leadership" path is that there may be a result in the end.[64] One caveat should be mentioned. The implicit leadership strategy will require clarity, commitment, and determination on the part of the United States. Without these, hemispheric integration will never be attained.

Appendix 2
Properties of NAFTA Models

Model	Model Characteristics
Single-Country Static CGE Models	
Levy and van Wijnbergen (World Bank)	Static CGE model of Mexico; detailed treatment of agriculture, income distribution, and agricultural policies; tradable/nontradable specification
Sobarzo	Static CGE model of Mexico; focus on imperfect competition and economies of scale in manufacturing sectors; Armington specification; in one version, the balance of trade is fixed and the exchange rate adjusts; in two other variants, the exchange rate is fixed and the balance of trade adjusts
Multicountry Static CGE Models	
US International Trade Commission	Highly stylized, two-country (United States and Mexico), CGE model; Armington specification for tradable good
KMPG Peat Marwick	Three-country CGE model (United States, Mexico, and rest of world); competitive markets; Armington specification
Hinojosa and Robinson	Three-country CGE model (United States, Mexico, and rest of world); competitive markets; policies represented by tariff, tax, and subsidy equivalents; Armington specification

Sectoral Structure	Factor Markets	Migration
Seven sectors focusing on maize and agriculture; one nontraded sector, one industrial sector	Two land types (irrigated and rainfed), capital, urban labor, and rural labor	Rural-urban migration. Depends on real income differential between rural and urban workers
Twenty-seven sectors, of which twenty-one are traded; one agricultural sector	Captial and labor; sectoral capital stocks and the wage are fixed in two versions, while in third the wage is flexible and capital is intersectorally mobile	Implicit rural-urban migration, as labor can move from agriculture to other sectors
Two sectors, a tradable and a nontradable	Capital and two labor categories, skilled and unskilled; capital is sectorally fixed	International migration of unskilled workers, using an elasticity of migration with respect to international wage differential
Forty-four sectors, focusing on manufacturing; four agricultural sectors	Capital and labor; fixed wage in Mexico	Implicit rural-urban migration, as labor can move from agricultural sectors to other sectors; no international migration
Seven sectors, with one agricultural sector	Land, capital, and four labor categories, various assumptions about factor mobility	Rural-urban migration within Mexico, Mexican-US migration for rural and urban unskilled labor; migration depends on wage differentials

Model	Model Characteristics
Multicountry Static CGE Models	
Robinson and others	Three-country CGE model (United States, Mexico, and rest of world); competitive markets; explicit modeling of agricultural and trade policies in both countries; Armington specification
Brown, Deardorff, and Stern	Five-region CGE model, including United States, Mexico and Canada separately; monopolistic competition and increasing returns to scale in most tradable sectors; goods differentiated by producer rather than by country of origin
Roland-Host, Reinert, and Shiells	Four-country CGE model (United States, Canada, Mexico, and rest of world); increasing returns and average-cost pricing in some sectors; Armington specification
Dynamic CGE Models	
Levy and van Wijnbergen (World Bank)	Dynamic CGE model of Mexico; model of transition period (nine years) terminating with steady-state balanced growth; tradable/nontradable specification
Hinojosa and McCleery	Stylized, dynamic, two-country CGE model of Mexico and United States; tradable/nontradable specification
McCleery and Reynolds	Stylized, dynamic, two-country CGE model of Mexico and United States; tradable/nontradable specification; capital accumulation, with investment determined by savings

Sources: See text notes for complete sources of models.

Sectoral Structure	Factor Markets	Migration
Eleven sectors, with four agricultural sectors	Land, capital, and four labor categories, various assumptions about factor mobility	Rural-urban migration within Mexico; Mexican-US migration for rural and urban un- skilled labor; migra- tion depends on wage differentials
Thirty sectors, of which twenty-three are tradable; one agricultural sector	Capital and labor, both intersectorally mobile	Implicit rural-urban migration, as labor can move from agriculture to other sectors; no international migration
Twenty-six sectors, with one agricultural sector	Capital and labor, both intersectorally mobile; fixed wage in all three countries	Implicit rural-urban migration, as labor can move from agriculture to other sectors; no international migration

Sectoral Structure	Factor Markets	Migration
Seven sectors focusing on maize and agricul- ture; one nontraded sector, one industrial sector	Two land types (irri- gated and rainfed), capital, urban labor, and rural labor	Rural-urban migration, depending on real in- come differential be- tween rural and urban workers
Two sectors, one traded, one nontraded	Capital and two labor categories: "high wage" and "low wage"; land is in- cluded in Mexico	Mexican-US migration depends on real in- come differential; some linkage between the two labor markets within both countries
Two sectors, one traded, one nontraded	Capital and two labor categories: "high wage" and "low wage"; land is in- cluded in Mexico	No migration; some linkage between the two labor markets within both countries

NOTES

1. For a discussion of the agreement and its implications, see Steven Globerman and Michael Walker, *Assessing NAFTA: A Trinational Analysis* (Vancouver: Fraser Institute, 1993); Gary C. Hufbauer and Jeffrey J. Schott, *NAFTA: An Assessment* (Washington, D.C.: Institute for International Economics, 1993); Luís Rubio, *¿Cómo Va a Afectar a México el Tratado de Libre Comercio?* (Mexico: Fondo de Cultura Económica, 1992); United States International Trade Commission, *Potential Impact on the U.S. Economy and Selected Industries of the North American Free-Trade Agreement*, Publication 2596 (January 1993).

2. Section A draws heavily on Nora Lustig, *Mexico: The Remaking of an Economy* (Washington, D.C.: Brookings Institution, 1993), chapter 5.

3. In addition to the licensing system, the government introduced domestic content requirements in the automobile sector in 1962 and so-called manufacturing programs designed to enhance the production of heavy intermediate products and capital goods.

4. For a historical overview of industrial policy, see Jaime Ros, "Mexico's Trade and Industrialization Experience Since 1960: A Reconsideration of Past Policies and Assessment of Current Reforms," paper prepared for the August-September 1991 UNU/WIDER conference in Paris; Gerardo Bueno, *Policies on Exchange Rate, Foreign Trade and Capital* (Mexico: El Colegio de México, 1987); Adriaan Ten Kate and Bruce Wallace, *La Política de Protección en el Desarrollo Económico de México* (Mexico: Fondo de Cultura Económica, 1979); Rene Villarreal, *El Desequilibrio Externo en la Industrialización de México (1929–1975): Un Enfoque Estructuralista* (Mexico: Fondo de Cultura Económica, 1976); Gerardo Bueno, "The Structure of Protection in Mexico" in *The Structure of Protection in Developing Countries*, ed. B. Balassa et al. (Baltimore: Johns Hopkins University Press, 1971); CEPAL-NAFINSA, *La Política Industrial en el Desarrollo Económico de México* (Mexico: NAFINSA, 1971).

5. Ros, "Mexico's Trade and Industrialization Experience," 6.

6. Ibid., 11.

7. Ibid., 15–19.

8. This information was leaked to the *Wall Street Journal* by unidentified sources. "U.S. and Mexico Agree to Seek Free-Trade Pact," *Wall Street Journal*, March 27, 1990, pp. A3 and A22.

9. The incorporation of Canada into the negotiations should not be surprising. Once it was clear that a U.S.-Mexico FTA was likely, the Canadian government felt it was better to be a full partner in the negotiations. Given Canada's interest, the United States could not pro-

hibit its neighbor and partner from participating. Consequently, the Mexican government had to accept trilateral negotiations. Though Mexico never made its reluctance explicit, officials were wary that the inclusion of Canada would complicate the achievements of its main target: free trade with the United States.

10. Under "fast-track" procedures, Congress can only give a "yea or nay" vote on the final agreement, thus giving trade negotiators wider authority during the bargaining process.

11. See Sidney Weintraub, *Free Trade Between Mexico and the United States* (Washington, D.C.: Brookings Institution, 1984), for an insightful explanation of both countries' past reaction to the prospects of an agreement on free trade.

12. See Robert Z. Lawrence and Charles L. Schultze, *An American Trade Strategy: Options for the 1990s* (Washington, D.C.: Brookings Institution, 1990).

13. Until then, import duties for about 15 percent of the tariff items in Mexico were calculated based on official import reference prices, rather than on the goods' transaction value. In several cases the official price was set at a higher level than the product's fair market value, thereby introducing a form of "hidden" protectionism.

14. For a more detailed discussion of these agreements, see United States International Trade Commission, *Review of Trade and Investment Liberalization Measures by Mexico and Prospects for Future United States–Mexican Relations, Phase I: Recent Trade and Investment Reforms Undertaken by Mexico and Implications for the United States*, Investigation 332–282, Publication 2275 (April, 1990); and B. Timothy Bennett, "A US-Mexico Free Trade Agreement: Its Evolution, Likely Content, and Related Issues," report prepared for the Latin American and Caribbean Country Department, The World Bank (Washington, D.C.: SJS Advanced Strategies, November, 1990).

15. Bennett, "US-Mexico Free Trade Agreement," 3.

16. Ibid., 22.

17. Claudia Schatan, "Trade Bargaining: The Mexican Case," paper prepared for the February 1991 Industrial Development Research Council (SELA) workshop in Caracas, p. 22.

18. Bennett, "US-Mexico Free Trade Agreement," 33.

19. See Lustig, *Mexico: Remaking of an Economy*, chapter 2, for further discussion on this issue.

20. The government's expectations were that after the agreement in principle was signed with commercial banks in mid-1989, Mexico's creditworthiness would rise, and capital repatriation and foreign direct investment would follow.

21. The commitment to form a regional free trade zone by December 1996 is part of the "Agreement of Tuxtla" signed by Mexico and the five Central American nations on January 11, 1991.

22. Colombia, Mexico, and Venezuela signed a Commitment to negotiate a FTA that would go into effect January 1992 during the "Guadalajara Summit" July 18, 1991.

23. For example, in 1991 Mexico signed a "framework agreement" with the European Community and began to seek membership at the OECD.

24. Aslan Cohen, "United States–Mexico Trade Relations" (Washington, D.C.: Inter-American Dialogue, 1990), 3.

25. Sidney Weintraub, *Marriage of Convenience: Relations Between Mexico and the United States* (London: Oxford University Press, 1990), 75.

26. Michael Hart, *North American Free Trade Agreement: The Strategic Implications for Canada* (Washington, D.C.: Institute for Research on Public Policy, 1990), 68–69.

27. United States International Trade Commission, 4–3; and Weintraub, *Marriage of Convenience: Relations Between Mexico and the United States*, 80.

28. For 1988 and 1989, almost 10 percent of U.S. imports from Mexico entered under the GSP. United States International Trade Commission, *Review of Trade and Investment Liberalization Measures by Mexico and Prospects for Future United States–Mexican Relations, Phase II: Summary of Views and Prospects for Future United States–Mexican Relations*, Investigation 332–282, Publication 2326 (October 1990), Table D–1, p. D–6.

29. Bennett, "A US-Mexico Free Trade Agreement," 31–32. For a discussion of the *maquiladora* program, see United States International Trade Commission, *Review of Trade and Investment Liberalization Measures by Mexico and Prospects for Future United States–Mexican Relations, Phase I: Recent Trade and Investment Reforms Undertaken by Mexico and Implications for the United States*, 5–13 to 5–18.

30. For example, brooms (38.6 percent), glass (38 percent), footwear (37.5 percent), and melons (35 percent). U.S. duties exceed 20 percent on 117 items. See Cohen, "United States–Mexico Trade Relations," 9, 12.

31. Cohen, "United States–Mexico Trade Relations," 12. Agriculture, livestock, and forestry account for 66 percent of all imports subject to licensing; oil and derivatives for 27 percent; and automobiles and parts for 6 percent.

32. The following are the specific goods subject to restrictions: wool tailored suits, trousers, skirts, shirts, acrylic fibers, and cotton webs in the textile category; tubes, wires, metal sheets, and special steels in the steel category; and avocados, potatoes, milk products, and sugar products in the agricultural category. See Cohen, "United States–Mexico Trade Relations," 12.

33. Weintraub, *Marriage of Convenience: Relations Between Mexico and the United States,* 81.

34. Michael Hart, "Elementos de un Acuerdo de Libre Comercio en América del Norte," in *México Ante el Libre Comercio con América del Norte,* ed. Gustavo Vega Cánovas (Mexico: El Colegio de México, 1991), 339–40.

35. Hart, *North American Free Trade Agreement: The Strategic Implications for Canada,* 71–75.

36. On the role of ideas, see Paul Romer, "Idea Gaps and Object Gaps in Economic Development," paper prepared for the February 1993 World Bank conference "How do National Policies Affect Long-run Growth?" in Washington, D.C.

37. Some authors call them applied general equilibrium (AGE) models.

38. Drusilla K. Brown, "The Impact of a North American Free Trade Area: Applied General Equilibrium Models," in *North American Free Trade: Assessing the Impact,* ed. Nora Lustig, Barry P. Bosworth, and Robert Z. Lawrence (Washington, D.C.: Brookings Institution, 1992), 26.

39. An exception to this were the "structuralist" general equilibrium models, which introduced the notion of imperfect competition by assuming mark-up pricing instead of market clearing in some of the sectors.

40. Drusilla Brown, Raúl Hinojosa, and Sherman Robinson provide two excellent summaries of their findings. See Drusilla Brown, "The Impact of a North American Free Trade Area: Applied General Equilibrium Models"; and Raúl Hinojosa and Sherman Robinson, "Labor Issues in a North American Free Trade Area," in *North American Free Trade: Assessing the Impact,* 26–57 and 69–97.

41. The Armington structure was introduced to accommodate the fact that prices of seemingly equal products varied from country to country (by a margin greater than that associated with transportation costs).

42. The Trela and Whalley model also has another distinctive feature: the bilateral quotas on steel, textiles, and apparel are not modeled

using ad valorem equivalents (as in the rest of the models); the model is solved incorporating quantitative restrictions that may or may not be binding.

43. That is, when all inputs are increased in a certain proportion, output must increase in the very same proportion.

44. See the discussion presented by Brown, "The Impact of a North American Free Trade Area: Applied General Equilibrium Models," 42.

45. That is, an increase in inputs results in a more-than-proportional increase in output; or, the average cost for the industry falls continuously.

46. Roland-Holst and others assume two alternative pricing behaviors: the contestable solution, which implies that firms price at average total cost and thus, since the latter declines monotonically, there can only be one firm in each industry; and the Cournot solution, which implies that firms set their profit-maximizing price assuming that the output of all other firms is given.

47. As Brown notes, there are several ways of introducing dynamic considerations in a model. See Brown, "The Impact of a North American Free Trade Area: Applied General Equilibrium Models," 50–51.

48. In addition to the dynamic models presented in Table 2.5, Kehoe's calculations suggest "that liberalization today could raise Mexican output per worker in twenty-five years by 51 percent above what it otherwise would have been" (ibid., 50) and McLeery shows that free trade would raise Mexican welfare by 1 percent by the year 2000 (starting in 1993), or if one allows for the impact of an agreement on investor confidence, Mexico's gains rise to 3.2 percent of GDP in the year 2000 (ibid., 56).

49. Timothy J. Kehoe, Comments to "The Impact of North American Free Trade Area: Applied General Equilibrium Models" by Drusilla Brown, in *North American Free Trade: An Assessment of the Impact*, 59.

50. In addition to CGEs, there have been other attempts to quantify the impact of NAFTA. Hinojosa and Robinson call them "extrapolation-regression models." Of those, Hufbauer and Schott predict a rise in Mexico's employment of the order of 2 percent by 1995 and INFORUM finds that employment in Mexico may decline by 0.5 percent. For a discussion of the characteristics and limitations of such approaches, see Raúl Hinojosa-Ojeda and Sherman Robinson, "Labor Issues in a North American Free Trade Area," in *North American Free Trade: An Assessment of the Impact*, 78–88.

51. Yet after fifteen years trade in agricultural goods between Mexico and the United States will practically be free, a major accomplishment indeed.

52. Although this negative impact could in principle be dampened through a combination of policies geared to the agricultural sector, in practice it could be very difficult to put them in place. Interestingly, in the actual NAFTA, corn is one of the sectors included under the longest liberalization schedule (15 years). Maybe the model results had some influence, or maybe it was a coincidence.

53. See Anne O. Krueger, Comments to "Labor Issues in a North American Free Trade Area," by Raúl Hinojosa-Ojeda and Sherman Robinson, in *North American Free Trade: Assessing the Impact*, 98–101. This issue is of great concern among Mexican policymakers and analysts. An interesting discussion is provided by D. Oks and S. Van Wijnbergen, *Mexico after the Debt Crisis: Is Growth Sustainable?* (Washington, D.C.: World Bank [mimeo], 1992). Unfortunately, there are no conclusive studies that would indicate which interpretation is accurate.

54. See Michael Piore, Comments to "Labor Issues in a North American Free Trade Area," by Raúl Hinojosa-Ojeda and Sherman Robinson, in *North American Free Trade: Assessing the Impact*, 101. One author has noted that in the past the dramatic effects of integration have been seriously underestimated by economists. Such underestimation is exemplified by Tibor Scitovsky's 1950s prediction that the benefits of integrating Europe would be of the order of 1–2 percent of its GDP. (See Carlos Bazdresch, Discussion in *North American Free Trade: Assessing the Impact*, 250–52.) The estimation procedures have improved since then. However, many of the more important so-called dynamic and intangible (confidence-enhancing and uncertainty-reducing) effects are still left out. Thus, perhaps one should view the quantities presented below as some sort of lower bound of what can be expected from the process of integration, in particular for Mexico, the smallest of the three economies.

55. See Krueger, Comments, 98–101.

56. See ibid., and Robert Z. Lawrence, Comments to "North American Free Trade Area: Applied General Equilibrium Models," by Drusilla Brown, in *North American Free Trade: Assessing the Impact*, 63–66.

57. In principle, the countries have a way to protect themselves from sudden import surges within the terms of agreement in NAFTA.

58. Carlos Alberto Primo Braga, "NAFTA and the Rest of the World," in *North American Free Trade: Assessing the Impact*, 210–34.

59. Refik Erzan and Alexander Yeats, "U.S.-Latin American Free Trade Areas: Some Empirical Evidence," in *The Premise and the Promise of Free Trade in the Americas*, ed. Sylvia Saborio (New Brunswick: Transaction Publishers, 1992), 117–46.

60. For a discussion, see Roberto Bouzas and Nora Lustig, "Apertura Económica, Integración Subregional y la Iniciativa para las Américas," Serie de Documentos e Informes de Investigación, Programa Buenos Aires, FLACSO, no. 132 (July, 1992), 1–51.

61. See, for example, Carsten Kowalczyk and Ronald J. Wonnacott, "Hubs and Spokes and Free Trade in the Americas," Working Paper 4198 (Washington, D.C.: National Bureau of Economic Research, December 1992); Richard G. Lipsey, "Getting There: The Path to a Western Hemisphere Free Trade Area and Its Structure," in *The Premise and the Promise: Free Trade in the Americas*, 95–114; Robert Z. Lawrence, "Escenarios Sistémicos para el Futuro del Comercio Mundial," *Pensamiento Iberoamericano*, no. 20 (July–December 1991); Anne O. Krueger, "Comments on a Free Trade Agreement with Australia," in *Free Trade Areas and U.S. Trade Policy*, ed. Jeffrey J. Schott (Washington, D.C.: Institute for International Economics, 1989); and the following papers prepared for the project "Support for the Process of Hemispheric Trade Liberalization," sponsored by IDB and ECLAC: Rudiger Dornbusch, "North-South Trade Relations in the Americas: The Case for Free Trade" (February 1993); Robert A. Pastor, "The North American Free Trade Agreement: Hemispheric and Geopolitical Implications" (January 1993); Sidney Weintraub, "Western Hemispheric Free Trade: Getting from Here to There" (November 1992); Anne O. Krueger, "Conditions for Maximizing the Gains from a Western Hemisphere Free Trade Agreement" (July 1992); and W. Max Corden, "A Western Hemisphere Free Trade Area: Possible Implications for Latin America" (May 1992).

62. See Kowalczyk and Wonnacott, "Hubs and Spokes and Free Trade in the Americas"; Lipsey, "Getting There: The Path to a Western Hemisphere Free Trade Area and Its Structure," in *Premise and the Promise: Free Trade in the Americas*, 95–114.

63. At present there are three members, but if NAFTA were to expand, so would the number of negotiating parties.

64. See Albert Fishlow, "Latin America and the United States in a Changing World Economy," unpublished manuscript, 1993.

THE MERCOSUL:
An Overview

Winston Fritsch and Alexandre A. Tombini

1. INTRODUCTION

On March 26, 1991, the Asunción Treaty was signed by four parties: Argentina, Brazil, Paraguay, and Uruguay. Later, on November 29, 1991, it was presented to the Latin American Integration Association (ALADI) under the legal framework of the "Acordo de Complementação Econômica (ACE-18)." This agreement set the framework for negotiating the establishment of the Common Market of the South (Mercosul) by January 1, 1995. If completed, this integrated market will encompass around 45 percent of Latin America's population, 60 percent of its total land area, and over 50 percent of the region's gross domestic product (GDP). In actual figures it will include a population of 197 million, an area of 11,863 thousand square km, and a GDP of US$515.68 billion (Table 3.1).

This chapter assesses the progress made during the first two years of a very tight negotiation schedule and looks towards future tasks. Section 2 describes both the genesis and the political economy of the integration initiative. In addition, it reviews the agenda for the negotiations, as consolidated in the presidential summit of Las Leñas, Argentina in June 1992. Section 3 takes a short-term standpoint, concentrating on the problems of the so-called "transition" period up to the end of 1994. It focuses on the feasibility of a minimalist agenda, comprising the formation of the customs union and rules for exchange-rate policy coordination.

Sections 4 and 5 look beyond 1994. Section 4 addresses the problems involved in completing the common market, which implies convergence towards deeper forms of integration in a longer time frame. Section 5 discusses the probable strategies of Mercosul

Table 3.1
Mercosul: Basic Indicators

Countries	Population (million)	Area (thousand km2)	GDP (US$ billion)
Argentina	33.1	2,767	112.05
Brazil	156.3	8,512	384.59
Paraguay	4.5	407	8.01
Uruguay	3.1	177	11.03
Mercosul	197.0	11,863	515.68

Note: The population and GDP figures refer to 1992.
Source: IDB, *Progresso Socio Econômico na América Latina 1992* and *International Financial Statistics*, August 1993.

towards the world trade system, both as a negotiating entity in the General Agreement on Trade and Tariffs (GATT), as well as when facing the challenges and opportunities of contemporary trends in discriminatory trade regionalization, especially within the Western Hemisphere.

2. The Genesis, Style, and Agenda of the Mercosul

There can be little doubt that the drive towards integration by Argentina and Brazil, which began in the mid-1980s, was the prelude to the Asunción Treaty. This momentum resulted from two great changes experienced by these countries in the 1980s: the transition to democracy and the redesign of corporatist patterns of government intervention, notably in the realm of trade policy.

These changes were not simultaneous, however. The overthrow of the military regimes preceded (by a good six years in Brazil) the shift towards trade liberalization. Early movements toward integration during the Alfonsín-Sarney era[1] were animated by a strategic political commitment that used simultaneously regained democratic institutions to foster amiable relations between the two countries, after many years of geo-political rivalries and potential conflict.[2] Still in the framework of repressive import regimes, these movements gave rise to an integration strategy designed in the old ALADI mold, one which was fit for the tra-

ditional inward-looking framework of industrial and trade policies and based on sectorally managed preferences, backed by
industrial promotion efforts to bring about negotiated regional
specialization patterns through so-called "complementarity"
deals.

A big shift in the design (and thus the feasible pace) of
integration between Argentina and Brazil came immediately after
the presidential changes which brought Menem and Collor to
power, radically altering the framework of trade policies in both
countries. Brazil's decision, in March 1990, to embark on a full-
fledged trade liberalization program set the stage for overhauling
the existing integration agreement.[3] The selective opening of markets on a product by product basis was replaced by linear, across
the board, and automatic tariff reductions ambitiously aimed at
establishing a Customs Union by January 1, 1995, thus forming a
common external tariff and a common trade policy in relation to
third parties. This new approach, embodied in the Ata de Buenos
Aires (June 6, 1990) was formalized on December 20, 1990, as a
bilateral agreement in ALADI under the legal framework of the
"Acordo de Complementação Econômica 14" (ACE-14).

The signing of the Ata de Buenos Aires, followed by U.S.
President Bush's speech launching the Enterprise for the Americas
Initiative, provided the motivation—reportedly under Uruguay's
request (CEPAL, 1992, p. 17)—for a high-level meeting between
representatives of Argentina, Brazil, Chile, Paraguay, and Uruguay. The goal of the meeting, which took place in Brasília in
August 1990, was to discuss the idea of expanding the geographic
boundary of the Common Market to encompass the Southern
Cone. In spite of Chile's defection,[4] this meeting set the ground for
the Asunción Treaty creating Mercosul on March 26, 1991.

The Asunción Treaty represents the "constitution" of Mercosul during the transition period, scheduled to last until December 1994. The treaty itself was designed to be replaced by January
1995. As a benchmark treaty, it is comprised of contractual elements such as an automatic reduction in import tariffs within
Mercosul, a program for the elimination of nontariff barriers
(NTBs), the establishment of a common external tariff, and the
definition of a common trade policy.

Due to its temporary nature, Article 18 of the Treaty established that the contracting parties will call an extraordinary

meeting to define the permanent institutional framework of Mercosul and the formation of the decision process after 1994. The meeting has been scheduled for the second half of 1994.

In the interim of the transition period, the intergovernmental decisions are being channeled through two provisory bodies: The Conselho do Mercado Comum (CMC) and the Grupo Mercado Comum (GMC). The former is the political branch and the highest level within the hierarchy of Mercosul governing bodies. It is comprised of the presidents of the four member countries, as well as the ministers of economics and foreign relations. The latter is the executive branch which oversees the implementation of the Asunción Treaty, enforcing negotiation deadlines and decisions of the CMC and also adopting the necessary measures to comply with the terms of the treaty.

An advisory committee with representatives of the Ministry of Foreign Relations, Ministry of Economics (or equivalent) and the Central Bank, form the national section of the GMC. The technical apparatus of the GMC is composed of eleven working groups covering a broad spectrum of issues.[5] During the transition period, all decisions of the governing bodies of the CMC and GMC are made by consensus of the four contracting parties.

From the outset, the possibility of implementing this ambitious integration program in a relatively short time was a cause for concern. Any change in the basic principles set for the transition period requires approval by the four parliaments. This check, seen as a positive factor, gave great resilience to these basic principles, and, in turn, gave stability to the negotiating framework.

Even so, there was skepticism about the ability to reach the necessary level of policy harmonization for launching Mercosul in 1995. Fears stemmed from the scope and complexity of the negotiations at the Working Groups, and from the fact that Working Group decisions had to be unified and incorporated into national legislation.

These fears were allayed to a large extent at the II Presidential Summit in Las Leñas in June 1992. At that meeting, bold action was taken to quicken the pace of negotiations, by defining differentiated, but rigid time schedules for the different issues under negotiation. This action imparted a needed sense of urgency to the negotiations, helping to clarify issues, and more importantly, it provided a hierarchy of priorities towards a minimalist agenda. To assess the progress made at Las Leñas, it is necessary to classify and divide the various policies dealt with by the eleven working groups into four broad "issue groups," based on the stated priority to resolve them.

Group 1, relating to measures affecting the trade regime, defined as the combined commercial and exchange-rate regimes, comprises the key issues of economic policy harmonization and coordination that must be resolved to launch the customs union at the beginning of 1995.[6] Commercial policy harmonization concerns border procedures. Here, the main tasks before the negotiators are: (i) the elimination of residual NTBs and the design of the common external tariff, as well as of common (antidumping [AD]/countervailing duties [CVD]) and safeguard rules; (ii) the treatment of problems created by the existence of special customs areas (Export Processing and Free Trade Zones) within the integrated area; and (iii) the harmonization of administrative customs procedures, of export promotion policies, and of trade agreements with third countries. Measures which relate to the exchange-rate regime are comprised of simplified foreign exchange transactions within the integrated region and also exchange-rate policy coordination among member countries.

Group 2, equally a prerequisite for consolidating Mercosul in 1995, relates to the design of Mercosul's permanent governance framework beyond the formative "transition" period. The final institutions and decision-making procedures are to be decided in the final Extraordinary Meeting of the Council, scheduled for the second half of 1994.

Group 3 covers (i) the harmonization of nonborder regulations affecting trade, such as indirect taxes affecting trade flows, transportation regulation, technical standards and investment protection, and certain asset and services markets; (ii) the integration of the national energy and transport systems; and (iii) the convergence of the instruments and scope of promotion (industrial, technology, agricultural) and competition policies, which comprise the eventual "sectoral agreements" proposed by private sector interests.

Although the negotiations under Group 3 will have a strong bearing upon the locational advantages of production in different regions within the integrated area, they are not essential for launching the customs union. Therefore, their harmonization can be accommodated by a longer time frame.

Finally, Group 4, with the least urgency of all, relates to long-term aims of macroeconomic (fiscal and monetary) policy coordination and the harmonization of labor market and social security regulation.

The following sections of the paper discuss both the difficulties of integration and the likely scenarios for the evolution of the negotiations in each of these different dimensions.

3. THE KEY ISSUES TO 1994

The main challenges prior to January 1, 1995 relate to the convergence of the trade regime and the design of the permanent governance structure. As far as the trade regime is concerned, there should be little difficulty in eliminating the few residual NTBs applied at the border, in harmonizing administrative customs and foreign exchange transaction procedures, or in making Mercosul compatible with existing trade agreements with third countries. Moreover, the existing legal framework of GATT—of which all countries except Paraguay are longstanding members—enormously simplifies convergence in AD and CVD procedures. Indeed, in the IV Presidential Summit (July 1, 1993), the CMC approved the "Regulamento Relativo à Defesa contra as Importações que Sejam Objeto de 'Dumping' ou de Subsídios Provenientes de Países não membros do Mercado Comum do Sul," Decision 07/93, which embodies the common AD and CVD legislation.

The sensitive issues, however, relate to four main problem areas. The first is the design of the common external tariff. Resistance is expected against either (i) the trade diversion and other inefficiency losses created in the process of convergence to a common tariff, which may be higher than that existing in the country before the formation of the customs union, or (ii) the disruptive import penetration caused by convergence to a common tariff much lower than the one previously in force.

Thus, the height of the tensions in designing the common external tariff is linked to the extent of divergence among the tariff structures of member countries. Large absolute differences over a

broad range of products can increase the difficulties in the negotiations. However, the fact that the Mercosul countries have already embarked on substantial trade liberalization and greatly
simplified their tariff structures[7] helps convergence. Indeed, as can
be seen in Table 3.2, tariff differentials between the two larger
partners are not wide on a product by product basis.

Another factor that facilitated the process of negotiating the
common external tariff was the decision by the technical group of
Mercosul to make use of eleven tariff levels. This methodological
decision helped to accommodate tariff movements and in many
instances circumvented the necessity for large variations in rates.[8]

Moreover, the high-level decision taken at the III Council
Meeting (CMC) in late 1992, fixing maximum rates at 20 percent but allowing for exceptions for specific products (which could
face reductions in a longer time frame from 1995 to the beginning of 2001) further simplified the negotiations. The maximum
tariffs in the offers made by all partners in September 1992 were
already below 20 percent except for some peaks in the Brazilian
tariff. These high Brazilian tariffs pertained to cars (35 percent),
informatic goods (35 percent), fine chemicals (30 percent), consumer electronics (30 percent), and computerized machinery (25
percent).

Brazil's partners are pressuring for faster and deeper tariff
reductions in the producer goods subset (informatics, fine chemicals, and machinery) because they are not substantial producers of
these goods. There is less pressure on Brazil to liberalize its auto
tariffs because Argentina also produces autos and still applies
quotas (auctioning at a greater premium than 35 percent). The
assemblers in the auto sector, backed by active trade unions, are
likely to press for new forms of managed trade. In consumer
electronics, where production comes chiefly from Brazil's Manaus
Duty Free Zone, the strong lobby protecting the interest of producers located in the area, arguing in the name of regional development objectives, may get a longer time frame to adjust to the
maximum rate. In general, however, converging to a common
tariff for a great deal of products looks feasible.

Recent tariff reform in Argentina (May 1993) under the
"1993–95 Growth Plan" has reduced the import tariffs on machinery and informatic goods from 15 percent to 0 percent and
eliminated the 10 percent surtax. This has greatly increased the

Table 3.2

Frequency Distribution of Tariff Differentials
(Argentina minus Brazil rates)

Differentials	Frequency	Relative frequency(%)
[-35%, -20%)	27	0.5
[-20%, -10%)	186	3.8
[-10%, -5%)	209	4.2
[-5%, 0%)	355	7.2
[0%]	2,036	41.2
(0%, 5%]	1,211	25.5
(5%, 10%]	621	12.6
(10%, 20%]	296	6.0
(20%, 35%]	—	-

Note: Argentine tariff includes the surtax ("tasa estadística") imposed in October 1992. The Brazilian tariff is that in force before the last round of automatic cuts in mid-1993 which brought the maximum rate to 35 percent and the average rate to 14.2 percent. Source: Elaborated from raw data from Departamento Técnico de Tarifas (DTT), Brazil, as processed by Centro de Economía Internacional.

difficulty of reaching a common external tariff for these products. One possible solution, which has already been studied, is the payment of a compensation by the Argentine government to the Brazilian exporter. This compensation would aim to restore the preference margin of Brazilian goods until a common tariff is reached.

The second crucial problem resides in how to avoid rapid shifts in intrazone competitiveness, caused either by the impact of eliminating border distortions (tariffs and exports subsidies) or by large fluctuations in the bilateral real exchange rate upon the relative prices of domestic production and competing imports measured in a common currency. Indeed, for a given member country, these relative prices, which crucially determine the rate of import penetration (i.e., the share of imports on internal demand), can be written as:

$$eP^*(1-s)(1+t)/P \qquad (1)$$

where, e stands for the nominal bilateral exchange rate, P^* for the level of prices in the partner country, P for the domestic price level, and s and t, respectively, for the preexisting subsidy and the tariff rates applied to the imports from the partner country. If we denote RER as the real bilateral exchange rate, equal to eP^*/P, then equation (1) can be rewritten as:

$$RER(1-s)(1+t) \qquad (2)$$

that is, large shifts in intrazone competitiveness stem either from the elimination of high preexisting tariffs, changes in export subsidies, or wide fluctuations on the bilateral real exchange rate.

Changes in the two commercial policy variables—tariffs and export subsidies—should not provide cause for much alarm. As far as tariffs are concerned, one should add to the aforementioned arguments that average rates are relatively low for their elimination to cause substantial dislocation: Argentina, 11.6 percent; Brazil, 14.2 percent; Paraguay, 6 percent; and Uruguay, 15.7 percent. Moreover, as already noted, in the products where Brazil will face large cuts, its producers usually face no competition within Mercosul.

Contrary to hearsay, export promotion policies among Mercosul members—a longstanding instrument in all countries, except for Paraguay, which started later than the rest—exhibit great commonalty today. To a large extent, the convergence was the product of trimming down a number of early incentives from the late 1970s, especially under a U.S. threat of CVD application. Today, these schemes are comprised basically of tax expenditures relating to indirect taxes such as drawbacks and value-added tax (VAT) rebates. Export financing has also been provided, but always under very unstable conditions.[9] Thus, it seems that the end of export incentives for intrazone exports in 1994 will not have any fundamental effect on bilateral competitiveness. Where this should happen, it could be compensated by national tax policies. Indeed, the end of fiscal export subsidies on intrazone trade is a powerful incentive for the harmonization of trade-related taxes among members. Only after that is achieved can the more ambitious task of unifying trade promotion policies towards the rest of the world be pursued.

One crucial challenge is how to constrain the large fluctuations in the bilateral real exchange rate—a by-product of the unstable macroeconomic situations in Argentina and Brazil since the 1970s. As seen in Chart 3.1, since 1989 the bilateral real exchange parity between Brazilian and Argentine currencies have continued to display wide fluctuations. On the Brazilian side, there was a protracted real appreciation from 1987, when the authorities tried to fight the slide to super-inflationary levels following the collapse of the Cruzado Plan by, among other things, delaying adjustments in the exchange rate. This was followed by a real depreciation of the Cruzeiro during the Collor government. The changes occurred primarily because of dual concerns to sustain activity levels through exports after the collapse of domestic demand following the application of strong monetary and fiscal breaks and to alleviate adjustment costs of the trade liberalization program.

On the Argentine side, the sharp depreciation experienced during the 1989 hyperinflation was followed by a typical overshooting in the adjustment towards equilibrium levels in the second half of 1990. However, in April 1991, the Cavallo plan froze the nominal exchange rate when the real rate was still some 40 percent below the 1986–87 average. Because inflation—even measured as wholesale prices—did not converge towards the dollar inflation level during the early months of the Plan, its implementation was followed by further small appreciations of the reborn peso.[10] It is interesting to note, however, that since late 1991, the real bilateral parity landed at roughly the level previous to these totally uncoordinated policy shifts.

Movements in activity levels, on the other hand, differed markedly since late 1991. In particular, Argentina's output shot up to an impressive boom, with GDP growing 9 percent in 1992. Given the overvalued peso, this led to a yawning trade gap, as seen in Table 3.3. The political consequence of the growing trade disequilibrium was to diminish Argentine enthusiasm for Mercosul, as imports from Brazil, which represented 90 percent of Argentine imports from Mercosul in 1992, rose even faster than total imports.

It is important to stress, however, that this bilateral trade gap is not fundamentally a result of real exchange-rate movements. As

Graph 3.1
Cruzeiro and Peso Real Exchange Rates against the Dollar
and Bilateral Parity (deflated by wholesale prices)

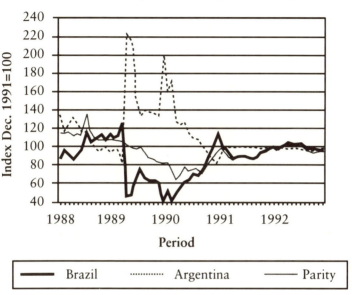

Source: Central Bank of Brazil and CEI

we have seen, the bilateral parity is not so out of line as to justify this, even allowing for commodity composition effects through differences in price elasticities of demand. The more reasonable explanation is twofold: first, relative activity level is an important factor, as the bilateral trade gap reflects the protracted Brazilian recession of 1992 and the fast recovery in 1993; second, integration hysteresis effects, caused by permanent changes in market structure following entrepreneurial decisions to adjust to the new business environment, constantly alter the equilibrium exchange rate.[11] Another contributing factor was the increase of oil imports by Brazil from Argentina, to a large extent resulting from the imposition of a 38 percent most favored nation (MFN) tariff on oil imports from third countries.

Irrespective of the causes for the slightly faster increase in Mercosul imports to Argentina, the present situation points to a

Table 3.3

Argentine Trade Balances: Global and Mercosul
(in millions of US dollars)

	1990		1991		1992		1993*	
	global	Mercosul	global	Mercosul	global	Mercosul	global	Mercosul
Imports	4,079	874	8,275	1,805	14,838	3,740	11,737	2,984
Exports	12,353	1,833	11,978	1,978	11,965	2,226	9,810	2,615
Trade Balance	8,274	959	3,703	173	-2,873	-1,514	-1,927	-369

*preliminary data from January to September.
Source: Instituto Nacional de Estadísticas y Censos

key problem for the common market: before sustainable price stability is regained in both countries, real rate bands are needed to sustain the process. Evolution from the targeted real exchange-rate band towards nominal targets can later be implemented, as stabilization succeeds on both sides of the border. However, the present small degree of trade interdependence between the two countries does not provide the incentives—as it does for the smaller partners in the European Community (EC) or those included in the North American Free Trade Agreement—to subordinate their exchange-rate policies to the integration objectives.[12]

As reviewed above, the wide variations in the real exchange rates of the peso and the Cruzado (Cruzeiro) in the past few years resulted from policy shifts based on purely domestic considerations. Only by chance was the bilateral parity kept roughly in line. This asymmetry requires that political will, and not economic self-interest, remain as the key driving force of the process.

This is a dangerous situation for at least two reasons. First, because Brazil is not willing—and correctly so—to abandon the allocation of the exchange rate for trade policy targets in the long run. And second, because Argentina has not yet decided whether or not it will defrost the peso-dollar exchange rate. Indeed, floating the peso is only one of the alternatives open to Argentina to consolidate the stability achieved so far. However, a shift to a crawling peg without reigniting inflation is only possible if accompanied by a social pact that reduces the chronic real wage resistance of the Argentine economy and calms asset markets. The other alternative is deflation brought about by recessive fiscal adjustment, which is probably better in the long run, as it may come together with an increase in public sector savings needed to sustain higher investment levels. Even so, a recession induced by a fiscal shock may create problems if the present tax structure is not altered, given the dependence of revenues on activity levels.

The political engineering of these alternatives is a daunting task, but time runs against the success of the Plan if the authorities stay put. It is already unlikely that the Argentine Central Bank will be able to finance the forecasted US$7 billion current account deficit without reserve losses in 1993. However, when the high prices of the nontradables eventually percolate to wage costs, a real appreciation will further damage competitiveness and is bound to lead to balance of payment strains and, eventually, an exchange crisis.

Certainly, the maintenance of the present situation is the single most serious threat to Mercosul. The Argentine trade imbalance has perverse political economy effects as it undermines the crucial preexisting support from Argentine industrialists for integration. The use of fiscal policy, such as the import surtax and additional tax rebates granted to exporters, to alter the "effective" (à la Bhagwati) exchange rate has clear limitations.

The third problem area of Mercosul centers around complications stemming from the existence of Export Processing Zones (EPZs) and Free Trade Zones within the region. Each country must live with tricky rules of origin to avoid the distortions introduced by the special trade regimes existing in the region. The difficult nuts to crack in the long run are: (i) how to inhibit the spread of further EPZs, especially in Brazil and Uruguay where local governments, whose importance has increased after the return to democracy, view these concoctions as a panacea for solving regional development problems; and (ii) how to wind down existing arrangements, backed by very concrete interests.[13]

Finally, the fourth problem issue is the building of permanent institutions. It is certain that some time down the road to the conformity of the Common Market, a supranational, active, competent, and committed bureaucracy will be needed (similar to the EC or OECD) to enforce the community rules. In the mean time, the required degree of supranationality has to be consistent with the concrete advances in the negotiating process in course.

By 1995, there will be some layers of supranationality related to trade matters. The remaining unfinished business will be carried over by an intergovernmental body, exactly as it has been during the transition period. This intergovernmental structure will continue to gradually conform, as the negotiations advance to the supranational framework of Mercosul. During the adjustment period, the national governments will have to be committed to the Mercosul project in order to respond to likely private-sector pressure for coordination of other (micro and macro) policies stemming from lower border barriers, and to fence sectorally localized protectionist pressures.[14]

4. BEYOND 1994 (I): THE LONG ROAD TOWARDS ECONOMIC UNION

The issue to be dealt with in this section is the convergence over time towards ample "jurisdictional integration" (Olson, 1965). In the short run (until the end of the century), the main task will be to harmonize nonborder incentives affecting locational advantages, as previously listed under issue Group 3. In the case of Mercosul, it may be possible to converge faster on these issues than did the EC due to the growing consensus on the framework of government intervention and thus, on the style of industrial policy reform. Forces for "deeper" integration in foreign direct investment (FDI), intellectual property, and technical standards are likely to prove irresistible over time. As some measure of independence in industrial promotion policies is usual in federations, convergence will still preserve some asymmetries in the pattern of intervention among members.

In the long term (beyond 2000), the key problems will shift to the consolidation of a broader economic unity: in this case, the main stumbling block will be the "bill" that Brazil's partners will need to pay due to regional differences in income levels (and general welfare conditions) between the Southeast and the very poor Northeast of Brazil. This problem is similar to the current EC problem of incorporating Eastern Europe. It basically boils down to the size of the fiscal transfers required to compensate for too wide a gap in average income levels. With integration, the present wide regional disequilibrium is, in fact, likely to increase due to the concentrationist effect of economies of agglomeration stemming from economies of scale, labor market pooling, and other forces generated in the industrial hub of the Mercosul, which perforce will lie south of Rio.[15]

The policy problems stemming from these trends may not be trivial. The politically easier way to tackle them, as mentioned previously, is through compensating transfers. This has indeed been the way it was "solved" in the Brazilian federation. Now, the question is to what extent Argentineans, Paraguayans, and Uruguayans will feel as responsible as Southern Brazilians in relation to the problem. This suggests that the fiscal union (an obvious requisite for monetary union) will probably be a thornier issue here than in the (relatively) more equalitarian Europe.

The alternative is labor mobility. This, however, may prove even less palatable at the present stage of the game. Indeed, up to now, the Mercosul agenda has been strictly dominated by business considerations. In fact, Working Group 11, which deals with labor relations, employment, and social security issues, was created as an afterthought, following the announcement of the other ten groups.

5. Beyond 1994 (II): Mercosul in the World Trade System

One should expect to see Mercosul prepared to act—as a negotiating entity in GATT[16]—in an aggressive defense of multi-lateralism as priority choice, but to take advantage of the oppor-tunities of regionalization. By virtue of the high commodity and market diversification of its exports, Mercosul could have a pos-itive role in furthering the GATT agenda on systemic issues (no-tably agriculture and the other backlog issues affecting tropical and manufactured goods) through alliances with other "systemic-oriented" global traders.

As far as "regional" or minilateral trade policy is concerned, hemispheric integration is the key issue in a two- to five-year time frame. This relates to a stand towards both NAFTA and the rest of South America.[17] On relations with NAFTA, given the still rela-tively high protection in Mercosul and the relatively small NAFTA share in total Mercosul exports, there is no great incentive for immediate accession even for Brazil, which faces by far the largest trade diversion losses. The most likely attitude of Mercosul nego-tiators is one of dealing with bilateral issues in the context of the 4 + 1 Group as they come up, especially in the key issues involving deep integration and technology transfer.[18] However, depending on the evolution of other Latin American accessions to NAFTA, trade diversion losses may increase the will to join. This is espe-cially true for Brazil which is a global trader with an export structure similar to that of the United States. The recent approval of Mexican accession by the U.S. Congress kept alive the hopes for a hemispheric integration.

South American integration should be an active policy objective for at least two reasons. The first is positive: if the continent returns to historical growth rates—as currently appears likely— under the more liberal trade regimes of the present, intraregional trade may accelerate rapidly, given the high share of manufactures in Mercosul exports to its neighbors. Moreover, in the long run, the development of efficient industrial systems and transportation networks are bound to make South America an increasingly integrated area. The second reason is defensive: to diminish the potential trade diversion losses of a hub-and-spoke pattern of NAFTA accession agreements with Mercosul's South American neighbors. This effect is actually small and will likely be eroded as multilateral liberalization proceeds.

How South American integration will be arranged is an open question to be addressed in the near future. It is likely, however, that small partners will resist the erosion of their preference margins in the Brazilian market, resulting from free trade between Brazil and her other South American neighbors.

NOTES

The authors would like to thank Honório Kume for helpful discussions of tariff issues and Arturo O'Connell for kindly providing data elaborated by the Centro de Economia Internacional (CEI).

1. Alfonsín was president of Argentina from 1983–89; Sarney was president of Brazil from 1985–90.

2. From the "Ata de Integração" (July 20, 1986), through Tratado de Integração, Cooperação e Desenvolvimento (November 29, 1989) providing for a common market by the year 2000.

3. The liberalization program was based on the abolition of non-tariff barriers (NTBs) followed by preannounced tariff cuts until the end of 1993 (later revised to mid-1993).

4. Chile's refusal to join, although based on arguments relating to the still relatively high levels of protection in Mercosul, was certainly also influenced by its attraction to the alternative of an early direct deal with North America. On Chile's trade policy strategy, see Meller (1992), and Butelmann's chapter in this volume.

5. Annex V of the Treaty defined the following eleven working groups: 1) Trade Matters; 2) Custom Procedures; 3) Technical Norms; 4) Fiscal and Monetary Policy; 5) Ground Transportation; 6) Water Transportation; 7) Industrial and Technological Policy; 8) Agriculture

Policy; 9) Energy Policy; 10) Macroeconomic Policy Coordination; 11) Labor Issues.

6. There will possibly be some exceptions to the Common External Tariff in 1995. For these products, a convergence schedule will be outlined for meeting the common tariff by January 1, 2001.

7. For instance, the number of tariff levels is equal to 5 in Argentina, 4 in Uruguay, 4 in Paraguay, and 8 in Brazil. The equivalent figure for the United States and European Community are 180 and 100, respectively.

8. By the end of 1993, Working Group 10 (SGT 10) had reached an "agreement in principle" for around 80 percent of the tariff universe.

9. For a thorough comparison of Mercosul's national export promotion regulations, see Guimarães (1992).

10. One should note, however, that the real peso rate, deflated by the consumer price index rather than by wholesale prices, appreciated much more as nontradable prices proved more sticky in reacting to the new nominal anchor. For a concise statement of the exchange-rate misalignments following the Cavallo Plan, see Frenkel (1992).

11. For a concise statement of the micro-foundations of this effect in a multilateral framework, see Baldwin and Krugman (1989).

12. At the July 1, 1993 meeting of the CMC, Brazil presented a proposal for real exchange-rate coordination within Mercosul.

13. The Manaus Free Zone, which sells over 95 percent of its output in Brazil, has benefits inscribed in the 1988 Brazilian Constitution that are effective for twenty-five years.

14. On this, see Motta Veiga (1992). An important issue here is the danger of the so-called sectoral agreements degenerating into corporatist arrangements inhibiting competition in the unified market.

15. Cf. Krugman (1991). The extent of the regional income effects will depend on the common trade regime; the worst of both worlds for Northeast Brazil will be a protectionist Mercosul.

16. Indeed, Mercosul has already proved to be a viable coordinating mechanism for multilateral negotiations. During 1993, Mercosul made a unified global offer in the Uruguay Round (ceiling binding consolidation of 35 percent for manufactured goods), and successfully managed to coordinate bilateral negotiations with nonmembers, through the definition of simple and transparent guideline parameters for negotiations.

17. Some analysts and Mercosul diplomats place some emphasis on the possibility of special agreements with the EC. We do not subscribe to this optimism, not only because of the low geopolitical importance of Mercosul to the EC, but also because of the widespread "Monroeism" to be found in Brussels.

18. The "4 + 1 Agreement" was signed on June 19, 1991 between the countries of Mercosul and the United States of America. It provides the institutional framework for the exchange of information between Mercosul and the USA.

REFERENCES

Baldwin, R., and P. Krugman. 1989. "Persistent Effects of Large Exchange Rate Shocks." *Quarterly Journal of Economics* (November).

CEPAL. 1992. *Panorama Reciente de los Procesos de Integración en America Latina e Caribe*, LC/R.1189, September, CEPAL, Santiago de Chile.

Frenkel, R. 1992. "La competitividad internacional de la industria argentina." *El Economista* 20 (October 1992).

Guimarães, E. A. 1992. "Sistemas e Instrumentos de Estímulo às Exportações nos Países do Mercosul." FUNCEX, Rio de Janeiro, mimeo, December.

Krugman, P. 1991. *Geography and Trade*. Cambridge, Mass.: MIT Press.

Meller, P. 1992. *Estrategia Comercial Chilena para la Década del 90: Elementos para el Debate*. Santiago, Chile: CIEPLAN.

Motta Veiga, P. da. 1992. "Abertura Externa e Integração do Mercosul: cenários para o período de transição." *Revista Brasileira de Comércio Exterior* (July–September 1992).

Olson, M. 1965. *The Logic of Collective Action*. Cambridge, Mass.: Harvard University Press.

ELEMENTS OF CHILEAN TRADE STRATEGY:

The United States or Mercosur?

Andrea Butelmann

Over the last years major changes have occurred in the international scenery that would not have been predictable a decade ago. Some of these changes are distinctly economic; others originate from altered political equilibria. But all of them contribute to create a new international economic landscape. Chile, a country integrated into the world markets and exposed to their ups and downs, must identify these changes and the new opportunities they open up to make policy decisions that will enable the country to avail itself of the benefits these changes present.

In the 1990s the conditions differ substantially from those prevailing fifteen years ago when the unilateral liberalizing process of Chilean trade started. Since then, most of the Latin American countries have agreed to set in motion a less protectionist strategy, and the discussion focuses on which is the best way to open up to the international markets. Several alternative liberalizing strategies exist: unilateral liberalization, liberalization within the frame of a customs union, and free-trade agreements (FTA). The latter grant each member country the freedom to establish its trade policy toward the rest of the world. In most of the Latin American countries the reduction of protectionism has occurred in a unilateral way by resorting to bilateral strategy as a complement to trade liberalization.

This new attitude of the Latin American countries toward the options of commercial policy has taken place at the same time that Chile recovers a democratic regime. The change in the political situation enables Chile to become accustomed to the new integration patterns and to attempt to establish connections with neighboring markets. In the 1980s the importance of Latin American countries in total Chilean trade diminished due to the recessions and the adjustment processes which Latin America underwent after the debt crisis.

At the time the countries of Latin America begin to adopt the liberalizing policies that developed countries have promoted for years, future viability of the world trade system is uncertain. The stagnation of the Uruguay Round of discussions of the General Agreement on Trade and Tariffs (GATT) questions whether this is the most suitable institutional mechanism to solve current problems affecting international trade through multilateral actions. At the same time, bilateral and intraregional negotiations are arising as more efficient alternatives for solving commercial controversies, by reducing the number of sources for dissension. This suggests a trend toward regional economic blocs.

The entrance of Eastern European countries into the international market also presents opportunities and challenges for Latin America. Chile must now compete in the developed markets of Europe against East European countries that have similar endowments of natural resources, but an added advantage of geographic proximity.

Within this context of intense change, Chile must consider an additional variable as it designs its trade policy for the 1990s. Through the Enterprise for the Americas Initiative, the United States has proposed a free-trade area for the entire continent. As time goes by, it becomes clearer that this is a long-term goal whose attainment depends greatly on the political climate in the United States, and on the progress Latin American countries make in their reform processes. Despite all of this, the possibility that Chile could sign a free-trade agreement with the United States is somewhat less distant.

Of these changes in the international scenery, two alternatives stand out that do not necessarily exclude each other. Chile must evaluate them carefully to ascertain the benefits each may offer. One alternative is to negotiate an FTA with the United States, which historically has been Chile's major trading partner. The other is to seek a greater integration with natural partners in close geographic proximity; that is, with member countries of the Southern Common Market (Mercosur). It is noteworthy that

Argentina and Brazil represent about 60 percent of Chilean trade with the countries in the Latin American Integration Association (LAIA).

This paper analyzes some of the issues that will be a part of the debate on the advantages and disadvantages of an FTA with the United States and the alternative trade strategies to which Chile can resort. The first section reviews the structure of Chilean exports in order to establish which integration alternatives are more suitable to comply with policy objectives. The second section lists the requisites a change in Chilean trade policy must satisfy. The third section examines various issues of a potential FTA between Chile and the United States or Chile's inclusion in the North American Free Trade Agreement (NAFTA). The fourth section reviews the projected advantages of Chile's association with Mercosur. The final section presents some conclusions.

I. Composition of Chilean Exports

The composition of Chilean exports to other countries is an important element in evaluating integration alternatives. Two dimensions will be considered in examining the structure of Chilean exports. First, exports are classified in three categories: natural resources (NR), industrial goods corresponding to processed natural resources (PNR), and other industrial products (OIP). Second, four destination markets are considered: the United States, the European Economic Community (EEC), Japan, and Latin America (LA).

The composition of Chilean exports to developed countries is fundamentally intensive in NR; in 1991 more than 61 percent of total exports to the United States and Japan, and nearly 70 percent of exports to the EEC, corresponded to NR (see Table 4.1). The PNR are the second item of importance in Chilean exports to these developed countries, accounting for close to 30 percent of total exports to each market. Together, NR and PNR account for more than 90 percent of Chile's total exports to these developed countries. The OIP share to these markets is marginal, representing 10 percent or less of total exports. In contrast, the composition of Chilean exports to Latin American Markets in 1991 presents a more balanced distribution for the three categories of goods: NR (35 percent), PNR (38 percent) and OIP (27 percent).

Table 4.1

Composition of Chilean Exports by Market of Destination,
1991 (percentages)

Sector	US	EEC	Japan	LAIA
Natural Resources (NR)	61.2	69.1	62.3	34.7
Processed Natural Resources (PNR)	28.7	26.3	36.4	38.0
Other Industrial Products (OIP)	10.1	4.6	1.3	27.3
Total (%)	100.0	100.0	100.0	100.0
Total Exports (Millions US$)	1,596	2,881	1,644	1,239

Source: Campero and Escobar (1992).

Considering the different volume of exports to the four regions, it is useful to examine the relative importance of each region
in the categories of Chilean industrial exports (Table 4.2). In 1991
the EEC and Japan were the destination markets for 26.6 percent
and 21 percent, respectively, of the total Chilean exports of PNR,
whereas the United States and Latin America represented around
16 percent each. Of the total OIP exports, 38.3 percent went to
Latin America, 18.2 percent to the EEC, 15.2 percent to the United
States, and 2.5 percent to Japan.

Over the past few years the composition of Chilean exports
has shifted; the rate of increase of processed exports has been
higher than that of unprocessed NR (see Table 4.3). When comparing the evolution of Chilean exports to the developed countries
over the period 1986–1991, Campero and Escobar (1992) observed a negative correlation between the sectoral exports of NR
and the PNR industrial equivalent according to a given destination
market. During this period forestry NR exports to the United
States dropped while forestry PNR increased significantly. Something analogous occurred with fishery and livestock RN. This
suggests the possibility of substituting NR exports by corresponding PNR exports in the same destination market; this, in turn
could increase the value added to the exported NR.

This analysis of the composition of Chilean exports suggests
that the Chilean comparative advantage with respect to the developed countries is in the NR, and that any increase in exports of

Table 4.2

Sectoral Distribution of Chilean Exports by Destination Market, 1991 (percentages)

Sector	US	EEC	Japan	LAIA	Rest	Total (%)	Total (Mill. US$)
NR	18.4	37.4	19.3	8.1	16.8	100.0	5,319
PNR	16.1	26.6	21.0	16.5	19.9	100.0	2,849
OIP	18.2	15.2	2.5	38.3	25.8	100.0	881
Total	17.6	31.8	18.2	13.7	18.7	100.0	9,049

Source: Campero and Escobar (1992).

Table 4.3

Average Growth Rates of Chilean Exports by Sector, 1986–1991 (percent per year)

Sector	U.S.	EEC	Japan	LAIA	Total
NR	9.5	13.4	25.3	4.0	13.9
PNR	13.1	16.5	47.8	11.1	18.0
OIP	28.9	37.8	42.0	44.5	35.8
Total	11.8	14.9	31.4	12.6	16.3

Source: Campero and Escobar (1992).

industrial goods to these markets should likely be oriented to the expansion of the corresponding PNR for current RN exports to each market. In the Latin American market, Chile has relatively balanced comparative advantages in all three export sectors.

II. Goals of Chilean Trade Strategy

In order to evaluate the options of commercial associations open to Chile, it is necessary to bear in mind the objectives of the Chilean trade policy. Although economic agents differ somewhat in their opinions, it is possible to list some general objectives on which there is broad consensus:

1. Increasing access: Because Chilean tariffs today are relatively low, not much can be gained in terms of a reallocation of resources by further reducing the flat 11-percent tariff. The objective is now to gain further access to foreign markets in exchange for additional reductions.

2. Stability in access: Chilean exporters are starting to see the negative consequences of their success. As exports increase, the threat of further limitations in access seems more concrete. Even if trade barriers remain untouched, the trend for countries to form trade and economic blocs threatens to displace Chilean exports from some markets. To secure the markets it has already conquered, Chile will need to join trade blocs that offer an invitation.

3. Diversification of markets and goods: The degree of stability both in macroeconomic terms and for specific sectors can be enhanced by higher degrees of diversification.

4. Second stage in exports: Diversification by itself does not seem to be enough. Many sectors of opinion prefer a certain type of diversification that is called the "second stage in exports." Although it is not easy to accurately define this objective, the primary goal is to promote exports that add more value to Chile's natural resources. This is becoming an objective of Chilean trade and economic policy, but some argue that it should not be a policy objective since it is occurring naturally. Three main arguments against this position exist: a) there is nothing wrong with exporting natural resources; b) it is good to add value, but we are already doing so, since industrial exports are increasing faster than those composed by unprocessed natural resources; and c) most of the natural resource exports have demanded that Chile develop sophisticated techniques qualitatively similar to industrial processes. Despite differences of opinion, there is consensus that Chile's trade policy should attempt to eliminate external barriers to industrial exports which are, in general, higher than those applied to raw materials.

Achieving these objectives is restricted by some prerequisites. Because macroeconomic stability is an established economic goal, any trade arrangement should assure that macroeconomic stability will not be at risk. At the same time, Chile needs to maintain an independent trade policy toward the countries not included in the trade strategy it chooses. A drastic change in tariffs toward third countries would cause a painful structural adjustment and lower trade if tariffs are raised. Furthermore, any trade agreement could cause more trade diversion costs than originally expected, and it is useful to be able to reduce tariffs to third countries to reduce those costs.

III. CHILE AND THE UNITED STATES

The possibility of signing a free-trade agreement with the United States is perceived as a positive event for the Chilean economy. Nonetheless, it is necessary to bear in mind that such an agreement will not generate spectacular benefits in terms of increased export access to that market, because protectionist barriers are already relatively low. In 1991 the weighted average tariff affecting Chilean exports to the United States was only 1.8 percent. Furthermore, these exports were practically unaffected by quantitative barriers; the greatest problems of access derived from technical barriers. Since then, some of these technical barriers have been solved by the bilateral committee.[1] Others, such as marketing orders for fruit exports, are unlikely to be eliminated in the negotiation of an FTA.

It becomes necessary, then, to explain the enthusiasm that has arisen in Chile concerning the possibility of negotiating an FTA with the United States. Several reasons exist; some are commercial in nature and others, though more intangible, offer benefits that could greatly exceed those afforded by the traditional effects.

A. Tariff Escalation and the Evaluation of Trade Effects

The fact that the average tariff levied on Chilean exports is minimal reflects the nature of Chile's exports: natural resources with no important degree of processing. In general, these goods are scarcely protected by the U.S. tariff system. However, studying the structure of the U.S. tariff system in detail reveals a strong tariff escalation in some sectors to protect the domestic industry. Thus, some Chilean products are affected by tariffs of up to 35 percent, and the tariff system includes tariffs that are higher for some other

Table 4.4
Tariff Escalation for Chilean Exports to the United States, 1990

| | TARIFF | | % Total |
	MFN	GSP	Exports
Agriculture			
Vegetables			
Fresh	9.5	6.4	0.52
Dehydrated	5.5	0.8	0.76
Frozen	17.5	14.4	0.03
Canned	13.8	13.6	2.26
Fruit			
Fresh	0.9	0.9	29.66
Dehydrated	2.0	1.9	0.53
Frozen	9.9	4.7	0.20
Canned	7.1	6.9	1.80
Fishery			
Fish			
Fresh	0.02	0.00	5.79
Frozen	0.01	0.00	2.62
Smoked	4.47	4.47	0.07
Canned	5.90	0.01	0.52

items (Butelmann and Campero, 1992). To the extent that Chile continues the successful process of diversifying its exports (see Section I), this escalation will become an important obstacle.

Tariff escalation is a very important topic at this moment in Chile, when the country is attempting to find mechanisms to attain the so-called second stage in the exports process, whereby a greater content of value added would be built into the exports of natural resources.

Table 4.4 provides an idea of the tariff escalation that affects Chilean exports to the United States. Escalation occurs in the four

Table 4.4 *continued*

	TARIFF MFN	GSP	% Total Exports
Forestry			
Timber			
Lumber	0.00	0.00	1.56
Agglomerates and Moldings	1.48	0.00	0.48
Wooden Articles	6.80	0.00	0.27
Wooden Furniture	3.20	0.00	0.68
Cellulose			
Cellulose	0.00	0.00	0.58
Paper	4.80	0.00	0.04
Copper			
Non-refined and refined	1.00	1.00	15.63
Alloys, bars, wiring and plates	1.20	0.00	1.57
Copper Articles	3.60	0.00	0.02

Source: Butelmann and Campero (1992)

sectors of interest to the Chilean economy but, in most cases, it disappears in relation to the tariffs regulated by the Generalized System of Preferences (GSP). Unfortunately, the escalation persists in Chile's primary export sector, i.e., agriculture. Furthermore, GSP is not guaranteed to last forever; as a matter of fact the program is reviewed periodically and can be canceled. In addition, countries become excluded, or "graduate," as their per capita income rises. Even if a country remains a beneficiary, particular products can be denied tariff preferences if the country is an important provider of those products. This is the case of Chile and its copper exports, both nonrefined and refined.

The tariffs shown in Table 4.4 are only a weighted average and, as such, do not reflect the degree of escalation of the products with little or no representation. Graphs 4.1 and 4.2 show the GSP tariffs for processed resources and for unprocessed resources on selected products of the agricultural and fishery sectors, respec-

Graph 4.1
Tariffs In The Agricultural Sector
(GSP)

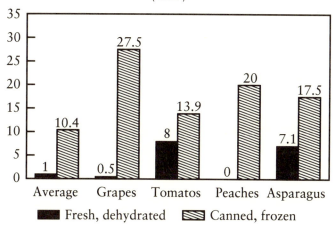

Graph 4.2
Tariffs In Sea Products Sector
(GSP)

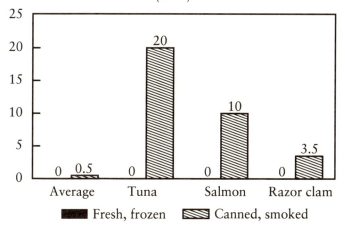

tively. It can be noted, that for selected products, the penalty on value-added is greater than that of the average for the sector. Thus it is necessary to make a product-by-product analysis in order to foresee the effects of a trade liberalization.

In summary, the elimination of tariff escalation, which would originate from an FTA with the United States, would have some effect on the composition of Chilean exports. This escalation alters the estimates of the commercial effects of an FTA. Obviously, the greater effect on trade will be generated on those goods having a higher initial protection. The problem in estimating trade effects for such goods is that, at present, virtually none are exported. Consequently, if a percentage of increase on such a small initial amount is applied, the effects of an FTA are underestimated.

The above explains in great part the difference in the results of two separate estimates made by Valdes (1992) and Erzan and Yeats (1992). The predicted results obtained by Valdes for the overall effects on trade of an FTA between Chile and the United States (with 1990 considered as the base year) are: (1) Chilean exports to the United States would increase by 4.4 percent (slightly more than US$60 million); (2) Chilean imports from the United States would increase by 27.5 percent (about US$375 million), of which 16.3 percent would result from creation of trade and 11.2 percent from trade diversion; and (3) the effects of these changes in terms of welfare would be equivalent to a net gain (using an intertemporal discount rate of 10 percent) of 1 percent of the GDP (approximately $310 million).

In contrast, Erzan and Yeats, who used a similar methodology, estimate an increase in exports of 2.8 percent. This is because they used trade information from 1986 when the diversification of Chilean exports and the percentage of processed goods, which are subject to higher tariffs, were lower.[2]

B. Other Effects

Several aspects of an FTA with the United States would benefit Chile. As stated in the previous section, perhaps the least important would be improved access of Chilean exports to the U.S. market. The tariff barriers in 1991 averaged only 1.8 percent and, even though a tariff escalation is present, a greater part is eliminated by the Generalized System of Preferences.

The great enthusiasm among Chilean authorities about the possibility of signing an FTA with the United States is based on benefits that are difficult to measure but are deemed to be far more important than a simple reduction of tariffs on current exports. It is crucial to consider that diversification of Chilean exports is growing and that barriers that are of no concern for us today could limit the growth of exports in the near future.

In this process of diversifying exports, which demand high levels of investment, stability of rules of access is a crucial aspect. Chilean producers need safeguards against surprises in matters of barriers to their exports and should barriers arise, producers need direct channels to solve any resulting controversies. This is important because, in the past, whenever exporters to the U.S. market became successful, protectionist pressures were exerted against them.

Protection against the access privileges attained by its major competitors will also benefit Chile as it gradually begins to export goods positioned at higher levels of protection. For an important percentage of exports, Chile's primary competitors in the U.S. market are Mexico and Canada. Since those countries will have unrestricted access to that vast market under NAFTA, as well as the existing advantage of being so close, it is important that Chile obtain similar conditions with regard to protectionist barriers.

Over and above the direct or potential benefits an FTA may have on trade flows, the mere fact of signing the agreement is strategically important. Even though Chile has negotiated other agreements and has signed an FTA with Mexico, an agreement with the United States offers Chile something no other agreement with Latin American countries is able to do. An agreement with the United States would include a much broader array of issues than a treaty with any other country and, with respect to each, the demands for transparency and predictability in the rules of the game will be far more exacting. Furthermore, the conditions established by the United States to sit at the negotiating table are a priori stricter than those of less developed countries. These requirements, which in some cases will be costly (as in the case of the environmental measures), will vouch for Chile's quality and enhance its ability to attract foreign investments at a time of intense competition among developing countries.

What will Chile pay for these benefits? It will face the traditional cost of an FTA: trade diversion. The participation of the United States in Chilean foreign trade has been decreasing; in 1991 it was below 18 percent. Thus, the possibilities of trade diversion are important, although the level of protectionism in Chile is low.

Chilean tariffs are (with some exceptions) at a flat 11 percent. However tariff reductions as considered within an FTA are gradual and Chile may continue to lower its tariffs for the rest of the world. As the preferential tariffs to the United States go down in conjunction with the general tariffs, the costs of trade diversion decrease. This cost would be even lower as other countries in the region join an hemispheric FTA.

Chile has already implemented a series of economic reforms to liberalize its internal markets and its foreign trade. Additionally, Chile has made important progress regarding international commitments. Due to these reforms, many people in both Chile and the United States believe the negotiation of an FTA will be relatively easy. However, some topics in the negotiation are bound to be complex. In addition, Chile will need to implement changes in the legal framework of foreign trade and in other laws and institutions. Following are several areas of possible conflict that will require, at minimum, a change in modus operandi:

Non-tariff barriers. Some agricultural products are exempted from the flat tariff regime. Wheat, oil seeds, oil, and sugar are subject to a regime of price bands designed to protect them from transitory fluctuations in international prices, but not to isolate the internal price from longer-term trends in the world markets. These price bands are implemented through variable duties. Other products, such as rice and flour, are protected by temporary surcharged tariffs. In the negotiations of an FTA, the United States will certainly exert pressure to lift these barriers. Chilean producers, of course, will oppose any plan to reduce the protection to the agricultural sector.

Subsidies. Chile has two systems of drawbacks. One of them, the so-called *simplified* drawback, applied to low-volume nontraditional exports is rebated as a percentage of the exported value and not in relation to imported inputs used, thus becoming in several cases a subsidy to exports. The elimination of both systems for exports to the United States is a potential source of conflict.

Government purchases. Chile would not need to introduce any great changes in government purchases since it currently abides by the principle of minimizing costs rather than of protecting national industry. However, this principle should be explicitly written into law and appeal mechanisms should be created to deal with cases of discrimination in assigning public tenders. The signing of the Government Purchases Code and its enforcement are important steps toward the transparency of the allocations in this sector. Chile has made a commitment to sign this code at the Uruguay Round negotiations.

Safeguard provisions. In an FTA between Chile and the United States, Chile is more likely to use emergency protection measures against sharp increases in the imports of a good that could negatively affect national industry. To do so, it would have to enact a law of safeguards. At present, changes in tariffs need Congressional approval, except in cases whereby protection is given against distortions in international prices that negatively affect national producers. In other words, Chile does not have the appropriate legislation to implement any agreement in safeguards reached in an FTA.

Compensatory and anti-dumping tariffs. One of the key arguments supporting an FTA with the United States is to ensure protection against the frequent compensatory and anti-dumping measures applied by that country. However, up to now, no country has managed to get the United States to modify its legislation in this regard. The most significant attainment has been to ensure that these decisions can be appealed at a bilateral panel. In this way, the appeal is subject to a more expedient and impartial process.

Existing Chilean legislation does not establish any difference between dumping and subsidies, and the procedures for setting up a tariff to provide protection against disloyal competition are not clear. Thus, to set up a binational panel to ensure that compensatory measures conform to the laws of the country imposing them, Chile will need to adjust some of its laws.

Investment. Though the Chilean regime regulating foreign investment is among the most liberal and nondiscriminatory in the world, it must yet modify some provisions—in particular, those that the United States has identified as a barrier for foreign investment. These relate to the transparency of the procedures for approving investments and the minimum time period to repatriate the capital invested. At present, the Foreign Investments Committee is empowered to reject foreign investment projects. Even though the committee has rarely exercised this right, it is necessary to regulate its use and the periods in which it may be exerted, because it introduces a degree of uncertainty in the approval process. On the other hand, the standing legislation does not provide for the repatriation of the capital until three years after the investment was actually effected. This restriction will be modified since a law to lower the period for the repatriation of capital to one year was recently enacted.

Intellectual property rights. Chile clearly will be under pressure during the negotiations to modify its intellectual property rights law, particularly regarding pharmaceutical patents. Only recently, under pressure exerted by the United States, did Chile adopt a new intellectual property rights law. However, the law did not satisfy the United States, as it established a period of protection for patents below what was desired and did not include a pipeline mechanism.[3]

Environment. Chile will have to take positive actions concerning environmental conditions. Though possibly beneficial in the long run, these actions will involve a high level of public and private spending.

In summary, although the direct benefits to Chile of an FTA with the United States will be minimal in the short run, public opinion regards such an agreement as protection against future negative events and as positive for the country's image. Even though the FTA will oblige Chile to make changes entailing costly investments, many believe those changes would have to be adopted sooner or later to maintain the country's international position and, therefore, the costs are not specific to an FTA with the United States.

VI. CHILE AND MERCOSUR

The United States has indicated that Chile is the only Latin American country ready to negotiate an FTA. This bodes well for Chile's image, but it denotes a postponement of the most important global benefits of the Enterprise for the Americas Initiative. It suggests that the United States will not advance quickly toward the ideal of having one single market from Alaska to Tierra del Fuego that would guarantee Chile free access to the markets of neighboring countries that have a great growth potential. A hemispheric agreement would offer Chile the opportunity to export industrial goods and to further diversify its exportable products (Sáez, 1992).

If that possibility is too remote, Chile will need to explore other mechanisms for expanding exports to those markets. One possibility is to join Mercosur. Created in 1991 by Argentina, Brazil, Paraguay, and Uruguay, Mercosur has set December 1994 as the deadline for finalizing the Common Market. This will involve (1) a schedule to eliminate tariffs and non-tariff barriers among the four member countries, (2) establishing a common external tariff (CET), (3) harmonizing norms and legal frameworks related to foreign trade, and (4) coordinating sectoral and macroeconomic policies.

Argentina and Brazil are Chile's two most important Latin American trade partners. Table 4.5 shows the magnitudes of Chilean trade with these two countries. Although exports to Brazil and Argentina represent approximately 40 percent and 18 percent, respectively, of Chilean exports within Latin America, they account for only slightly more than 8 percent of the country's total exports.

Chilean authorities have hesitated to join Mercosur for several reasons. First, these countries have not been able to attain macroeconomic stability. Second, the Mercosur countries have agreed to have a common external differentiated tariff with a higher maximum rate than the 11 percent that Chile maintains. Chile experienced the costs of deep structural change when it opened to the international markets in the 1970s and is not willing to face another acute change in either relative prices or long-run incentives. Furthermore, adopting a common external tariff would eliminate Chilean trade policy independence. It would increase the difficulty of negotiating FTAs with other regions, would delay the negotiation of an FTA with the United States, and would leave no instruments to reduce trade diversion in case it exceeds anticipated levels in the integration process with Mercosur.

Not only is Chile's position unfavorable toward Mercosur, but no one knows if the possibility is even open for Chile to join. Despite the fact that the Mercosur Treaty contains a provision that makes affiliation possible for other LAIA member countries, applications for participation will only be considered five years after the actual enforcement of the treaty. Exceptions will be granted to

Table 4.5

Chilean Trade with Argentina and Brazil

	ARGENTINA			BRAZIL		
	Exports from Chile[a] (Millions US$)	Imports from Argentina[b] (Millions US$)	Exp. Chile to Arg. / Exp. Chile to L.A. (%)	Exports from Chile[a] (Millions US$)	Imports from Brazil[b] (Millions US$)	Exp. Chile to Brazil / Exp. Chile to L.A. (%)
1985	84	106	15.7	210	249	39.2
1986	161	123	23.5	293	248	42.8
1987	175	159	21.0	348	380	41.7
1988	168	279	19.3	342	555	39.2
1989	110	399	11.5	523	703	54.5
1990	114	503	11.2	487	564	48.0
1991	257	554	20.8	448	698	36.2

Source: Banco Central.

[a]Chilean Exports are FOB.

[b]Imports to Chile from Argentina and Brazil are CIF.

countries that "neither belong to sub-regional integration unions nor to extra-regional associations." This has been interpreted as a mechanism in the Mercosur Treaty specifically to enable the anticipated incorporation of Chile; when the treaty was signed only Chile fulfilled that condition and Argentina and Uruguay have repeatedly expressed their approval of incorporating Chile. However, since that time Chile has signed an FTA with Mexico and Venezuela and it may eventually sign an agreement with the United States.

Despite the disadvantages and problems associated with joining Mercosur, the enormous possibilities these markets offer cannot be disregarded. These countries are the main destinations of Chilean exports to Latin America, and they still have levels of protection higher than those of the United States.

Alejandra Mizala (1992) outlines alternative options that should be analyzed concerning the incorporation or nonincorporation of Chile to Mercosur. Chile's absence from Mercosur could displace competitive Chilean exports by those of trade partners who avail themselves of the tariff preferences. Considering the extreme case of retaining only copper exports, Mizala calculates that for the year 1990 Chilean exports to Argentina and Brazil would decrease by US$81.6 million and US$276 million, respectively. This represents a joint decrease of 4.3 percent of total Chilean exports. A less extreme scenario assumes that Mercosur would not affect all Chilean exports that are competitive with the reciprocal exports of the member countries of Mercosur. In this case, other exports in addition to copper would be retained and Chilean exports to Argentina and Brazil would decline by US$74.5 million and US$165.7 million, respectively. The negative effect on total Chilean exports would be about 3 percent.

Beyond avoiding these losses and making potential gains in trade, joining Mercosur could accelerate the flow of foreign investments. It is not enough for Chile to be a relatively efficient country with entrepreneurial skills, acquainted with the export business and with reliable rules on foreign investment. It is fundamental that there also be a market where the firms to be set up in the country can trade their products. Otherwise, Chile will continue primarily to attract foreign investors who will exploit natural resources for subsequent processing in their country of origin (see Tsunekawa, 1992). Clearly, companies will be more

keenly interested in availing themselves of the advantages offered
by Chile if, in addition to meeting the needs of the small internal
market, they are assured access to markets as important as those
of Argentina and Brazil. Attracting foreign investment on the basis
of an incentive involving larger markets is more difficult to achieve
through an FTA with the United States. This is because investments will be oriented to Mexico, which has relative geographical
advantages and also enjoys the advantage of having been the first
Latin American country to join NAFTA.

Hence, it seems important for Chile to design a strategy that
takes full advantage of the markets of Argentina and Brazil and,
simultaneously, minimizes the costs mentioned earlier. The central
issue is to achieve preferential access to these markets without
having to adopt the common external tariff. This is not a new
problem; on other occasions it has been solved by signing an FTA
with either a customs union or a common market. The question
arises whether the Mercosur countries would be interested in this
option. Argentina has shown interest in incorporating Chile as a
member of Mercosur, in part due to interest in acquiring greater
strength to negotiate a common external tariff lower than that
proposed by Brazil. But it is not clear whether the idea of an FTA
Chile-Mercosur will be supported.

Chile's leaders have not fully explored the alternative of
signing an FTA with Mercosur. The official Chilean position
toward Mercosur has been extremely cautious; however, toward
the end of 1992 there was a change of attitude in some government, entrepreneurial, and academic circles. In particular, the
entrepreneurial groups that had previously shown great skepticism
began to show interest in establishing contacts with Mercosur and,
in particular, with Argentina. The change in attitude no doubt
stems from the recent boom of Chilean investments in Argentina
following the economic reforms implemented by that country.[4]

At the same time, Chile has negotiated separate economic
complementation agreements with both Argentina and Brazil.
With Argentina tariffs were not an issue, but other barriers to
trade and investment were discussed before signing an agreement
in 1991. Negotiations with Brazil are still in process. That agreement may include a reduction in tariffs, although any rebate
granted by Brazil will have to be reviewed by December 1994

when Mercosur is fully enacted. In any case, these partial approaches pave the way for expanded integration in the future.

VII. SUMMARY AND CONCLUSIONS

From a Chilean perspective the possibility of an FTA with the United States is deemed positive. From the standpoint of trade alone, the effects would be moderate, with increased benefits for specific exporters such as the agro-industrial sector, whose present access to the U.S. market is limited by high tariffs.

In addition to tariff reduction, an FTA with the United States would require regulation of government purchases, nondiscriminatory treatment to foreign services, eliminating restrictions to foreign investment, protecting intellectual property rights, and so forth. Chile has implemented, or is in the process of complying with, most of these requirements. Nevertheless, it will be necessary to make important institutional changes to attain greater degrees of clarity and predictability, and also to create mechanisms to control these processes.

Negotiations with the United States serve a commercial purpose and vouch for Chile's ability to attract foreign investment. However, Chile should not neglect negotiation with Mercosur. The markets in those four countries are considerable in size, and assured access to them can be an important motivation for foreign investment. Chile today offers conditions of stability and nondiscrimination that have a great appeal, but it is not able to offer assured access to a wide market.

An FTA with Mercosur, in which Chile would maintain independence in its trade policy, would assure greater diversification of markets and products. Currently more than 60 percent of what Chile exports to the developed world is composed of unprocessed natural resources. In contrast, these products account for only 35 percent of exports to Latin America. These differences suggest that the two integration schemes would attract different kind of investments. An FTA with the United States, with exception for a few productive sectors, will likely expand investment in the traditional sectors. On the other hand, access to Mercosur would attract more investment to the industrial and service sectors.

NOTES

1. In September 1990, as a direct result of the launching of the Enterprise for the Americas Initiative, Chile and the United States signed a framework trade and investment agreement. In June 1991, a bilateral working group was set up to deal with bilateral trade issues. Some of the pending issues have already been solved in this context.

2. In absolute terms, the results obtained by Erzan and Yeats were US$22.8 million. When Valdes repeated this exercise with 1986 data, he obtained a result of $26.3 million.

3. The pipeline mechanism would have granted protection to those products patented before the law was enacted but which were not in the market at that time because of the long process of required testing.

4. It is estimated that Chilean entrepreneurs invested US$253 million in Argentina in 1991 and more than US$300 million in 1992.

REFERENCES

Butelmann, A., and P. Campero. 1992. "Medición del escalonamiento arancelario de las exportaciones Chilenas a los EE.UU." In *Estrategia comercial chilena para la década del 90: Elementos para el debate,* ed. A. Butelmann and P. Meller. CIEPLAN.

Campero, P., and B. Escobar. 1992. "Evolución y composición de las exportaciones chilenas, 1986–1991." In *Estrategia comercial chilena para la década del 90: Elementos para el debate,* ed. A. Butelmann and P. Meller. CIEPLAN.

Caves, Frenkel, and Jones. 1990. *World Trade and Payments: An Introduction.* New York: Harper Collins.

Erzan, A., and S. Yeats. 1992. "U.S.-Latin American Free Trade Areas: Some Empirical Evidence." In *The Premise and the Promise: Free Trade in the Americas,* ed. S. Saborio. Overseas Development Council.

Ffrench-Davis, R. 1985. *Economía internacional: Teorías y políticas para el desarrollo.* Mexico: Fondo de Cultura Económica.

INFORUM. 1991. "Industrial Effects of a Free Trade Agreement Between the U.S. and Mexico." Report by Interindustry Economic Research Fund for The United States Department of Labor.

Mizala, A. 1992. "Chile, Argentina y Brasil: Perspectivas de su integración económica." In *Estrategia comercial chilena para la década del 90: Elementos para el debate,* ed. A. Butelmann and P. Meller. CIEPLAN.

Sáez, R. E. 1992. "Chile y América Latina: Apertura y acuerdos bilaterales." In *Estrategia comercial chilena para la década del 90:*

Elementos para el debate, ed. A. Butelmann and P. Meller. CIEPLAN.

Tsunekawa, K. 1992. "Japanese Investment in Liberalizing Latin American Economies: Current Patterns and Possible Impacts of the FTA Initiatives." University of Tokyo (paper prepared for LASA, Los Angeles).

UNCTAD-WORLD BANK. 1989. *A User's Manual for SMART, Software for Market Analysis and Restrictions on Trade.*

Valdes, R. 1992. "Una metodología para evaluar el impacto cuantitativo de una liberalización comercial. Aplicación al ALC entre Chile y EE.UU." In *Estrategia comercial chilena para la década del 90: Elementos para el debate*, ed. A. Butelmann and P. Meller. CIEPLAN.

THE ANDEAN GROUP AND LATIN AMERICAN INTEGRATION

José Antonio Ocampo and Pilar Esguerra

I. INTRODUCTION

The revival of the largely dormant regional integration processes and the design of new schemes of intraregional trade have been outstanding features of recent trade reforms in Latin America. This is a somewhat paradoxical result, as integration schemes were designed in the region in the 1960s as instruments for limited trade liberalization and import substitution in an enlarged market. Until very recently liberal economists regarded them as distortions to free trade.

The Andean Group was created in the late 1960s and underwent a radical change in recent years when emphasis shifted away from the inward-looking notions which pervaded its initial conception toward intraregional trade liberalization. This process was facilitated by the convergence of all member countries towards open trade regimes. The Group is, indeed, one of the most advanced integration processes in the developing world: a free-trade zone is now in operation and a common external tariff should be in place by May 1994. Moreover, it includes a unique intellectual property regime, some common rules regarding services, and other features of more advanced integration processes. However, negotiations have become increasingly difficult and have revealed that trade integration—i.e., the ratio of intraregional flows to total trade—is still low compared to other integration schemes like the Central American Common Market or the Association of South East Asian Nations.

The Andean countries, particularly Colombia and Venezuela, have also been actively involved in negotiating new free-trade agreements with other nations in the continent. Both countries have already signed treaties with Chile and the Group of Three (involving them and Mexico), and are exploring a possible agreement with Central America. These negotiations have faced opposition from other members of the Andean Group, which regard them as violations of the multilateralism that should characterize negotiations by members of a customs union. However, Colombia and Venezuela have argued that Andean integration is only part of a larger process of trade liberalization and hemispheric integration and should be no obstacle to the subscription of new free-trade agreements.

This chapter summarizes ongoing integration processes in the Andean countries, giving particular attention to Colombia's involvement. Despite the important nontrade aspects of Andean integration, it focuses on intraregional trade. The chapter is divided in five sections, the first of which is this Introduction. Section II takes a brief look at the history of the Andean Group and its recent revival. Section III shows the evolution of intraregional trade in the Group. Section IV describes the main features of other free-trade negotiations. The final section draws some conclusions.

II. Institutional Developments in the Andean Group

The Cartagena Agreement, which gave birth to the Andean Group, was signed in 1969. As other integration schemes created in Latin America and other developing countries at the time, it was based on import substitution principles. In particular, it supported the view that, due to the economies of scale characteristic of the advanced phases of import substitution, this process could only take place in an enlarged market. According to this conception, such markets should continue to be protected by high tariffs and import restrictions from the rest of the world, as new instruments were designed to encourage the development of new import substitution activities and to guarantee that domestic firms benefited from such new industrial activities. The instruments of Andean integration were then: (1) a liberalization program, designed to generate restricted competition within the area; (2) a common external tariff, to protect the enlarged market against imports from the rest of the world; (3) the sectoral industrial development programs, to induce new advanced import substitution activities; and (4) a common policy towards direct foreign investment.

Throughout the 1970s, Andean trade grew vigorously (see Section III). However, this dynamism was only related in part to institutional developments.[1] Indeed, neither the liberalization program nor the rest of the institutional paraphernalia of the Group functioned well. The common external tariff was never approved, liberalization for competitive goods was systematically postponed, industrial development programs were designed only for a few sectors and proved cumbersome and operationally deficient— particularly due to the political criteria used to allocate new activities. Moreover, governments gradually abandoned the principles which initially inspired the Agreement, as Chile's breach in 1976 made particularly clear. However, this period coincided with favorable external factors (particularly the Venezuelan and Ecuadorian oil booms and the simultaneous Colombian coffee bonanza), which generated rapid income growth in most Andean nations.

In contrast, intraregional trade experienced a prolonged crisis in the 1980s as a result of the commodity and debt crises which afflicted all Andean nations (including Colombia, though to a moderate extent). All of them strongly devalued their currencies during the decade and imposed trade restrictions to correct their balance of payments deficits. By the end of the decade, the Andean Group was virtually collapsing due to the widespread transgression of the liberalization program by member countries and the total breakdown of industrial programs. In an attempt to avoid the final disintegration of the regional scheme, flexibility was introduced, including the postponement of existing obligations and the creation of such provisions as "administered trade" and "industrial complementarity agreements."

After 1989 the Andean Group received renewed political stimulus but was rapidly detached of its import substitution elements. Emphasis was placed on intraregional trade liberalization, the elimination of restrictive provisions regarding direct foreign investment and intellectual property rights,[2] and the design of complementary tools to trade liberalization, such as regional unfair trade legislation and free transportation in the area.

The December 1989 presidential meeting in the Galápagos Islands in Ecuador was the crucial turning point. In this meeting, the heads of state of Andean countries decided that the most restrictive provisions, such as administered trade, should be rapidly phased out, that a free-trade zone would be in place by December 1993 (1995 for Bolivia and Ecuador) with a small list of exceptions,[3] and a customs union established by December 1997 (1999 for Bolivia and Ecuador). The November 1990 presidential meeting in La Paz, Bolivia sped up the commitments with a decision to consolidate the free-trade zone by December 1991 for all members, and that the customs union would be in place by December 1993 (1995 for Bolivia and Ecuador). Although at the time Ecuador did not agree to the acceleration, at the May 1991 presidential meeting in Caracas, it decided to enter the free-trade zone in 1992.

In 1990 and 1991, the Colombian government faced strong opposition to the liberalization of the steel and automobile sectors in the Andean Group. This opposition was lifted when the presidents of Colombia and Venezuela agreed in March 1991 to create a three-year transitional program during which bilateral trade in these sectors would be subject to "industrial complementary agreements" between the private sectors of the two countries. This transitional mechanism was eliminated in early 1992 for the automobile sector and one year later for steel. Opposition continued and, indeed, increased in later years in some agricultural sectors, due to distortions generated by the lack of common import rules for oilseeds, cereals, milk, and other products[4] or those generated by Venezuelan production subsidies (rice). Nonetheless, the Colombian government has refused to reverse trade liberalization in any of these sectors. In August 1993, however, the presidents of Colombia and Venezuela signed special agreements to temporarily manage bilateral trade of rice and potatoes, which in both cases implies a degree of administered trade.

In the Caracas presidential summit in May 1991 and the November meeting of the Cartagena Agreement Commission (the assembly of ministers of foreign trade of the Andean Group), major differences surfaced among the Andean nations regarding three critical areas: the design of the common tariff, harmonization of export incentives, and rules for negotiating free-trade agreements with third countries. In the first of these areas, Colombia, Ecuador, and Venezuela defended an escalated but simple tariff structure, whereas Bolivia and Peru supported a flat tariff.

The Cartagena Agreement Board (the executive branch of the Andean Group) proposed a four-rate structure with rates of 5 to 20 percent. With respect to export incentives, there was basic agreement on the need to eliminate all export subsides to intraregional trade (except the drawback and equivalent mechanisms) but not with respect to the harmonization of export incentives vis-à-vis third countries. Colombia also requested that production subsidies be eliminated, but Venezuela has systematically rejected proposals on this matter.

The most controversial matter related to free-trade negotiations with third countries. The controversy was associated with two different issues: whether negotiations by members of a would-be customs union with third countries should take place on a bilateral or a multilateral basis, and the distortions in trade flows which could be generated by negotiating with countries that have free-trade agreements with third nations; the most important case is obviously Mexico, given that it is a member of the North American Free Trade Agreement (NAFTA).

With respect to the first of these issues, Venezuela and Bolivia strongly advocated allowing each member of the Andean Group to conduct bilateral negotiations with third countries; they believed an alternative procedure might slow down negotiations. On the contrary, Ecuador, Peru, and the Cartagena Agreement Board argued that negotiations should be conducted preferably by the Andean Group as a whole, allowing member countries to conduct negotiations on a bilateral basis only if other countries did not consider them beneficial. Colombia initially held an intermediate view on the matter, claiming that there should be some multilateral restrictions to bilateral trade negotiations with third countries and that they should include clauses allowing other Andean nations to participate in the benefits of these negotiations.

Nonetheless, Colombia soon joined Venezuela and Bolivia on this issue and, as a result, Andean countries have been free to undertake trade negotiations with third countries on a bilateral basis. Indeed, Peru's lack of commitment to the Group and the Group's delay in adopting a common tariff because of Ecuador's request for special treatment (see below), have led Colombia and Venezuela to look at Andean integration with growing distrust. They regard free-trade agreements with third countries as a way to force Andean integration to move faster or, alternatively, to break the limits that it may pose to consolidating larger free-trade areas.

The second issue in this controversy was equally important. It is well known that the absence of common tariffs and full harmonization of export incentives may generate distorted trade patterns within a free-trade area. The probability of such distortions is greater the more intricate the network of such agreements. For example, NAFTA will give Mexican firms access to U.S. intermediate goods at zero tariffs. This would place Colombian and Venezuelan producers at a disadvantage in the Group of Three, as the Mexican product would enter free of tariffs to those countries, thus forcing both nations to either reduce tariffs or sign competitive agreements with the United States. The dynamics of free-trade agreements thus generates the opposite behavior to the classical "beggar thy neighbor policy" of the 1930s. The only way to avoid this result would be stringent rules of origin, which are difficult to manage and may easily become an important nontariff barrier, offsetting the benefits from free-trade agreements.

In early December 1991, the Andean presidents' meeting in Cartagena temporarily resolved the political deadlock. The agreement reached in this summit included:

(1) The establishment of a customs union in January 1992, with a four-rate, escalated common external tariff (5, 10, 15 and 20 percent), except for a few basic raw materials subject to zero tariffs and cars which were allowed a maximum rate of 40 percent. The 20 percent tariff level would be brought down to 15 percent in January 1994, when the tariff for cars would be fixed at a unique 25 percent level.

(2) Due to its geographical isolation, Bolivia would continue to enjoy a special status, keeping its current tariff structure with only two rates (5 and 10 percent).

(3) Peru was allowed an additional six months to dismantle its list of exceptions, a similar treatment to that granted to Ecuador in May 1991. The residual list of exceptions would be eliminated in January 1993 except in the case of Ecuador, for which it would gradually be phased out from January 1993 to July 1994.

(4) Both export and production subsidies affecting intraregional trade would be phased out in January 1993 and export incentives affecting sales to third countries would be simultaneously harmonized.

(5) Negotiations with third countries would take place on a multilateral basis, particularly in the case of ongoing negotiations with Mexico in the context of the Group of Three. Chile and the Southern Common Market (Mercosur) would also be invited to negotiations with the Andean Group. Nonetheless, any country was allowed to undertake bilateral negotiations if approved by the Cartagena Agreement Commission.

Once again these decisions proved difficult to implement. The commission was unable to reach consensus on a common external tariff after intensive negotiations from December 1991 to February 1992. This led to a bilateral decision by Colombia and Venezuela in March 1992 to adopt a common tariff, covering slightly over 90 percent of the tariff schedule, but they did not reach an agreement for the remaining tariff items. As a result, and due to the lack of harmonization of the system of variable levies (price bands) for agricultural goods and the lack of uniform preferences granted to third Latin American countries, a full customs union has not been in operation even between these two countries.

Negotiations with the rest of the Andean Group remained stagnant until June 1992, blocked by two main obstacles. First, Ecuador demanded preferential tariffs for crucial inputs it does not produce. Second, in April 1992, Peruvian President Fujimori declared a self "coup d'état." This political event led Venezuela to suspend diplomatic relations with the Peruvian government, creating a conflictive political environment within the Group. In response, Peru suspended its trade liberalization obligations with all Andean countries.[5] In June 1992, this unilateral decision was replaced by a common agreement to allow Peru to stay temporarily out of the Andean Group.

In September 1992, Ecuador's decision to finally enter the free-trade zone breathed new life into the Group. Peru was allowed until December 1993 to decide whether it would continue to be an Andean Group member. At a March 1993 commission meeting in Bogota, the Cartagena Agreement Board presented a proposal for an escalated common tariff consistent with the criteria approved by the presidents in Cartagena in December 1991. The commission approved this proposal in Decision 335, and established that it would be in full operation in January 1994. However, because considerable differences regarding the common tariff still existed, Decision 335 also contained: (1) a preferential treatment for Ecuador, allowing a list of more than 1000 items with tariffs 5 to 10 points below the common tariff (Annex 2); (2) a group of items with zero tariffs, conformed by the list of goods that already had such a tariff in each country on March 2, 1993 (Annex 3); and (3) the compromise of presenting a reduced list of goods in which the countries would be allowed to dissent from the common external tariff (Annex 4).

It was decided that intensive negotiations would take place through the rest of the year to reach a full agreement on these three Annexes. In practice, rather than clarify the way in which the Andean customs union would enter in operation, Decision 335 brought a lot of confusion to the Group. In particular, the long list of preferences granted to Ecuador and the possibility of dissenting from the external tariff through Annex 4 worked against the adoption of a veritable external tariff.

As the new common tariff increases average nominal protection by over one percentage point, there has been strong opposition by some members of the Colombian cabinet to Decision 335. In order to solve this difficulty without recurring to Annex 4, since September 1993 Colombia carried out conversations with Venezuela to modify some basic rates agreed in Decision 335, bringing them back to rates currently in place in both countries. As a result, they have reached an agreement on most of the tariff schedule, in which average protection is only a few decimals from current national levels.

However, significant differences with Ecuador still remain. This country has not yet abandoned its traditional pattern of demanding preferential treatment within the Andean Group. In fact, in the last meeting of the Cartagena Agreement Commission, in December 1993, Ecuador presented a list of more than 1000 items as its Annex 4, on top of the long list of preferences already granted as Annex 2 of Decision 335. The countries decided to delay the implementation of the common external tariff four additional months, to analyze this proposal.

In addition to the common external tariff, some other instruments should be harmonized among the Andean nations to complete the design of the customs union. The most important is the special treatment given to some sensitive agricultural products through variable levies (price bands), which automatically increase (fall) whenever international prices fall (increase) below (above) a certain floor (ceiling) level. Colombia, Ecuador, and Venezuela have adopted this mechanism, but the list of goods included and the methodologies used to calculate floor and ceiling trigger prices differ among the national systems.

The ministers of agriculture of the Andean countries directly conducted the negotiations to harmonize price bands. After two years they finally reached an agreement in October 1993. It included a common methodology for calculating floor and ceiling prices and variable levies, and a list of 130 items covered by the system. However, the agreement later faced strong opposition by other members of the Ecuadorian and Venezuelan cabinets and, consequently, has not been approved by the Cartagena Agreement Commission. Although a domestic consensus was reached in Ecuador, this has not been true of Venezuela, and it is unclear what position the new Venezuelan government, inaugurated in early February 1994, will take on this and other outstanding controversies.

One of the outstanding items in the agenda is the elimination of drawback and similar export incentives for intraregional trade and the harmonization of export incentives with respect to third countries. The main reason this issue has been set aside in the negotiations is that, although export subsidies and drawback systems are incompatible with a customs union (as they create distortions in competitive conditions within the integration area), almost 60 percent of intraregional exports benefit from such mechanism. It is feared that eliminating this instrument may endanger the current intraregional trade boom.

Moreover, difficult negotiations still lie ahead regarding the harmonization of sectorial and macroeconomic policies. Based on discussions in recent years, Venezuela will strongly resist the dismantling of production subsidies. In Colombia, it is generally believed that Venezuelan authorities subsidize crucial industrial inputs, particularly electricity, iron ore, and basic petrochemicals, and that public-sector industrial firms have received massive subsidies from the central government. Venezuela systematically rejects these claims.

In the area of harmonization of macroeconomic policies, there have been some preliminary discussions, particularly between Colombia and Venezuela. However, harmonization will not advance in any significant way in the next few years, given the strong macroeconomic imbalances between some Andean members. It is also unlikely that countries will be willing to harmonize macroeconomic policies as long as intraregional trade does not represent a large share of total trade. As Figure 5.1 indicates, despite significant increases in recent years, the ratio of intraregional to total trade—which is referred to as the "integration coefficient"—was slightly under 8 percent for the Andean Group as a whole in 1992. Under these circumstances, it is even surprising that institutional developments have gone so far. A likely explanation to this paradox is that harmonization is a result of the convergence of trade policies rather than a reflection of a full commitment to Andean integration.

From this point of view, recent political developments in some countries, notably in Venezuela, that may lead to a reversal in liberalization policies, generate uncertainties regarding the future of the integration process. This factor will add to Peru's unwillingness to reestablish its Andean commitments and Ecuador's call for special treatment.

III. Evolution of Intraregional Trade in the Andean Group

The overall evolution of intraregional trade in the Andean Group is summarized in Figure 5.2 and Table 5.1. Three major periods can be differentiated. From 1970 to 1979, Andean trade boomed. It multiplied tenfold in nominal terms during this decade, growing at an annual rate of 29 percent, albeit from a fairly low base. The 1980s were dismal for Andean trade. After a slowdown in 1980–1982, it collapsed in the following years, reaching a minimum in 1986, when intraregional trade had halved with respect to the early 1980s. By 1989, when the Galápagos presidential summit took place, it was still below the level reached in the first years of the decade. With the consolidation of a free-trade area and overall liberalization, Andean trade has again boomed in recent years. Between 1989 and 1993 it tripled from under US$1 billion to US$2.8 billion. The average growth rate in this four-year period (34.5 percent) has, indeed, surpassed that of the booming 1970s.

Colombian exports to the Andean Group have shown a similar pattern (see also Figure 5.2). They boomed in the 1970s

Figure 5.1

Andean Trade: Integration Coefficients

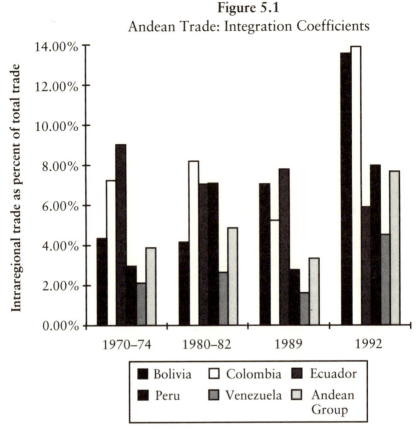

Source: Calculations based on Junta del Acuerdo de Cartagena.

but collapsed in 1983 and 1984, declining by 63 percent compared to the 1982 level. Although they partially recovered, the 1989 level was still 25 percent below the 1980–1982 level. Since 1989, exports to the Andean Group have increased at an annual rate of 41.4 percent, above the average rate of growth for the Andean Group as a whole.

The evolution of Andean trade has been affected by structural factors, such as the degree of complementarity in the productive structures of member countries, as determined by comparative advantage and past trade and industrial policies. For example, the traditional bias of Venezuelan industrial policy toward heavy manufacturing and Colombia's bias toward light

Table 5.1
Intraregional Trade (US$ Thousands)

Exporter Country	Importer Country					Andean Group	Trade Integration
	Bolivia	Colombia	Ecuador	Peru	Venezuela		
Bolivia							
1970–74		1,218	2,846	10,375	17	14,455	4.35%
1975–79		3,928	6,254	9,245	1,511	20,938	2.98%
1980–82		7,195	1,126	27,428	4,698	40,447	4.16%
1983–87		3,292	1,865	15,843	594	23,043	3.16%
1988		4,154	185	22,617	544	27,500	5.06%
1989		5,113	291	45,148	511	51,063	7.06%
1990		4,012	122	53,046	2,771	59,951	7.21%
1991		30,538	948	47,422	3,414	82,322	10.83%
1992		28,432	1,093	49,632	4,768	83,925	13.54%
Colombia							
1970–74	2,187		24,969	31,125	18,298	76,579	7.24%
1975–79	3,465		44,440	21,927	204,394	274,226	12.85%
1980–82	2,271		65,165	22,584	328,651	418,670	8.19%
1983–87	1,295		55,632	52,941	145,562	255,430	5.18%
1988	2,553		53,438	87,297	259,942	403,230	7.55%
1989	5,187		59,999	60,257	185,138	310,581	5.22%
1990	5,187		74,538	89,342	203,671	372,738	5.28%
1991	9,160		126,883	212,600	429,765	778,408	10.37%
1992	14,917		155,626	270,083	558,945	999,571	13.88%

Table 5.1 (continued)

Exporter Country		Importer Country				Andean Group	Trade Integration
	Bolivia	Colombia	Ecuador	Peru	Venezuela		
Ecuador							
1970–74	148	13,681		22,280	132	36,241	9.02%
1975–79	438	58,351		78,209	12,245	149,243	11.96%
1980–82	430	79,400		10,901	48,748	139,479	7.05%
1983–87	163	124,308		15,477	9,572	149,520	6.74%
1988	218	43,460		128,966	4,519	177,163	8.04%
1989	584	41,361		135,049	6,187	183,181	7.78%
1990	408	32,229		138,358	17,537	188,532	6.95%
1991	612	31,911		164,084	7,102	203,709	7.15%
1992	970	63,049		98,395	11,831	174,245	5.88%
Peru							
1970–74	3,503	12,100	5,973		6,305	27,880	2.96%
1975–79	30,692	31,127	39,004		30,906	131,730	7.11%
1980–82	41,748	100,709	51,878		49,842	244,177	7.09%
1983–87	14,968	57,396	27,570		89,959	189,893	7.81%
1988	9,100	40,094	13,500		72,330	135,024	5.01%
1989	4,580	38,000	18,000		37,000	97,580	2.76%
1990	19,961	94,666	31,743		54,522	200,892	6.22%
1991	22,100	113,600	47,467		86,267	269,434	8.09%
1992	26,809	79,368	41,967		117,470	265,614	7.96%

Table 5.1 (*continued*)

Exporter Country	Importer Country					Andean Group	Trade Integration
	Bolivia	Colombia	Ecuador	Peru	Venezuela		
Venezuela							
1970–74	23	9,776	25,436	23,545		58,780	2.12%
1975–79	126	92,156	6,611	66,166		165,059	1.74%
1980–82	525	293,177	21,309	20,884		335,895	2.64%
1983–87	300	235,288	9,347	30,694		275,629	3.12%
1988	774	170,782	16,329	53,357		241,242	2.39%
1989	349	160,979	19,966	28,519		209,813	1.61%
1990	570	390,190	67,833	35,081		493,674	2.83%
1991	626	309,091	69,433	85,790		464,940	3.12%
1992	815	469,905	42,444	119,188		632,352	4.51%
Andean Group							
1970–74	5,861	36,775	59,223	87,325	24,751	213,936	3.88%
1975–79	34,721	185,562	96,310	175,546	249,056	741,195	4.80%
1980–82	44,973	480,481	139,478	81,796	431,939	1,178,667	4.86%
1983–87	16,726	420,284	94,414	114,955	245,687	893,516	4.67%
1988	12,645	258,490	83,452	292,237	337,335	984,159	4.71%
1989	10,700	245,453	98,256	268,973	228,836	852,218	3.33%
1990	26,126	521,097	174,236	315,827	278,501	1,315,787	4.21%
1991	32,498	485,140	244,731	509,896	526,548	1,798,813	6.13%
1992	43,511	640,754	241,130	537,298	693,014	2,155,707	7.66%

Source: Based on data from the Junta del Acuerdo de Cartagena.

Figure 5.2
Evolution of Andean Trade 1970–93

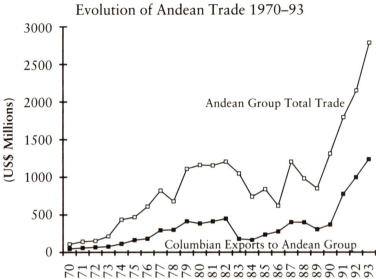

Source: Calculations based on Junta del Acuerdo de Cartagena Monthly Bulletins.

manufacturing have been major determinants of bilateral trade. To the extent that the liberalization program mainly affected noncompetitive goods before 1989, these factors were reinforced by trade policies. The main elements that have recently influenced intraregional trade have obviously been trade policies, and relative prices and incomes.

Given the nature of the liberalization process prior to 1989, there was a clear bias towards noncompetitive, intraregional trade flows. This included some degree of competitive trade in "late" industrial sectors such as chemicals and metal mechanic activities. Industrial development programs then in place also affected trade flows in late manufacturing activities. However, rapid income growth and improved transportation networks also generated some competitive trade flows. Overall, nontraditional exports dominated Andean trade and, indeed, the Andean Group made a significant contribution to the diversification of exports of most member countries. In 1980–1982, average nontraditional, intraregional exports were US$789 million, equivalent to 66 percent of intraregional trade and 28 percent of nontraditional exports of member countries (up from 14 percent in 1970 and 21 percent in 1975). Intra-industry trade also grew during these years, peaking at 25 percent of total intraregional trade in 1982, but then collapsed to only 9 percent in 1983.[6]

Through the 1980s, as intraregional trade stagnated, aggressive devaluation policies generated a boom of nontraditional exports to third countries. As a result, nontraditional intraregional exports declined to only 10–11 percent of total Andean exports. Nonetheless, intraregional trade continued to absorb a large proportion of exports of late manufacturing activities. For example, in 1989 44 percent of Colombia's exports of chemicals and 30 percent of those of metal products—i.e., of skilled-labor and technology-intensive activities—were mainly purchased by other Andean countries (Table 5.2). Compared to 1980, the strongest contraction of trade had been experienced by competitive exports (leather, apparel, and nonmetallic minerals, the latter included as "other capital-intensive" exports).[7]

With the recent boom, intraregional trade has experienced significant changes. The liberalization of competitive exports has led to expanded trade in traditional agricultural and manufacturing goods. Although no recent estimates are available, intra-industry trade has no doubt experienced a significant increase. Nonetheless, inherited differences in productive structures continue to play an important role in the determination of trade flows. Table 5.2 summarizes changes in the structure of Colombian exports to Andean countries. The recent boom has allowed, for the first time, a rapid increase in the exports of textiles and natural resource-intensive manufactures. Competitive exports of nontextile, capital-intensive manufactures (mainly nonmetallic minerals and paper) have also recovered, as have exports of metal products, both of which experienced a significant contraction in the 1980s. Overall, if 1992 exports to the Andean Group are compared to those in 1980, the largest increase has occurred in chemicals, textiles, and natural resource-intensive manufactures; whereas the former can be classified as noncompetitive, the latter two are certainly competitive exports.

All countries have benefited in terms of export growth from the recent Andean boom, though to a different extent. The most impressive phenomenon has been the growth of bilateral trade between Colombia and Venezuela. This was also a feature of the

Table 5.2
Colombian Manufacturing Exports to the Andean Group, According to Factor Intensity (US$ Thousand)

Factor Intensity	1980			1989			1992		
	Andean Group	All destinations	% to Andean Group	Andean Group	All destinations	% to Andean Group	Andean Group	All destinations	% to Andean Group
Natural resource intensive	59,714	353,704	16.88	38,877	402,447	9.66	164,228	654,022	25.11
Unskilled labor intensive									
Leather, apparel	70,565	94,441	74.72	40,954	173,402	23.62	61,874	399,811	15.48
Other	32,848	77,398	42.44	27,315	135,926	20.10	71,087	217,104	32.74
Capital intensive									
Textiles	19,218	121,013	15.88	14,192	139,929	10.14	79,054	287,511	27.50
Other	39,184	98,847	39.64	11,882	69,654	17.06	68,358	161,827	42.24
Skilled labor and technology intensive									
Chemicals	57,638	99,864	57.72	100,507	230,581	43.59	201,182	432,159	46.55
Metal products	84,194	143,689	58.59	37,343	122,908	30.38	164,824	369,015	44.67
Total	363,361	988,955	36.74	271,069	1,274,847	21.26	810,608	2,521,448	32.15

Source: José Antonio Ocampo and Leonardo Villar, "Fuentes de competitividad de las exportaciones industriales de Colombia," *Coyuntura Económica,* December 1993. Classification of goods according to factor intensity based on domestic sources.

1970s. Based on Table 5.1, it can be estimated that bilateral trade between these two countries had increased from 13.1 percent of intraregional trade in 1970–1974 to 52.8 percent in 1980–1982. As a result of the Venezuelan crisis, this proportion fell to 42.6 percent in 1983–1987 and 40.6 percent in 1989. In recent years, it has again increased to 47.7 percent in 1992 and 54.6 percent during the first three quarters of 1993. Both countries show above average growth rates in exports to the Andean Group.

This is also true of Bolivia, particularly if 1988 rather than 1989 is taken as the point of reference. In contrast, Peru and Ecuador have lagged behind. Despite overvaluation, Peruvian exports to the Group have increased, but imports have expanded at a much faster rate. As a result, this country has turned a traditional surplus in intraregional trade into a large deficit (see again Table 5.1). This helps explain Peru's difficulties with Andean integration. Ecuador's lag in adopting the new rules of Andean trade liberalization explains the relative stagnation of its exports during the first three years of the decade; in 1993, however, it had clearly joined the intraregional trade boom.

As a reflection of booming trade, integration coefficients increased for all countries, except Ecuador, between 1989 and 1992 (Figure 5.1). In the latter year, the highest coefficients were those of Bolivia and Colombia, which were close to 14 percent. Peru's coefficient was close to average and those of Ecuador and Venezuela were below average. This was a new phenomenon for Ecuador, whose integration coefficients had always exceeded the average level for the Group. Venezuela had always had the lowest integration coefficient for the Andean Group but, with the recent boom, nonoil exports of this country have become strongly dependent on intraregional Andean trade.

IV. Other Free Trade Negotiations

A. The Group of Three

In August 1990, the presidents of Colombia, Mexico, and Venezuela agreed to design the Group of Three, with the purpose of creating a free-trade area by the end of the decade. This agreement actually includes two bilateral treaties (Colombia-Mexico and Mexico-Venezuela), as Colombian-Venezuelan relations would continue to be ruled by Andean regulations. Although ambitious objectives were initially set up, opposition to the agreement mounted in each country, slowing negotiations. The change of the Mexican negotiating team in December 1992 (when the team that had been in charge of NAFTA took over) marked a new starting point and throughout 1993 negotiations sped up. After a declaration by the three presidents in October, negotiations accelerated so that a draft agreement was ready by November 1993. However, internal opposition in Venezuela postponed the final signing of the treaty. The new Venezuelan government is likely to request additional adjustments to the text and, indeed, the minister of foreign relations declared in mid-February 1994 that the Group of Three was not a priority for Venezuela.

Throughout the negotiation process, it was established that tariffs for noncompetitive goods and for some exportables of special interest to member countries would be brought to zero at the outset and that goods would be classified, according to the sensitivity to the different countries, in three additional lists, for which the periods during which tariff reduction would take place would be five, ten, and fifteen years. However, negotiations of the lists proved very difficult. Intensive participation of the private sectors of the three countries made negotiations even more complex. To break the deadlock, the presidents of the three nations decided in October 1993 that liberalization of all goods will take place simultaneously in a ten-year period. Only two sectors were excluded from this rule: automobiles and agriculture. These principles were included in the November 1993 draft text. It was, nonetheless, agreed that tariffs for goods covered by prior bilateral Latin American Integration Association (LAIA) agreements would be brought down to zero at the onset of the agreement.

Following LAIA principles, the draft accord includes some elements of nonreciprocity through the transitional period. In particular, it was decided that the speed of the tariff cut will be faster for Mexico than for Colombia and Venezuela. Mexico will start to liberalize its trade from its current tariff level minus 28 percentage points for all goods, whereas Colombia and Venezuela will start to cut their tariffs from the agreed Andean external tariff minus 12 percentage points.

Differences in agricultural policies made negotiations in this sector particularly difficult. Mexico recently adopted its new agricultural policy, *Procampo*, which establishes general subsidies for agricultural production, with the purpose of managing the effects of Canadian and U.S. subsidies on NAFTA trade. The variable levies for agricultural goods of Colombia and Venezuela were considered by Mexico throughout the negotiations as a nontariff barrier which should, thus, be turned into a tariff. Given differences in agricultural policies, it was finally agreed that "sensitive" goods in this sector would be excluded from the agreement. On the other hand, the automobile industry was considered as a highly sensitive sector by both Colombia and Venezuela, reflecting the significant differences in competitiveness with respect to Mexico. Tariff reductions for this sector will take place during a twelve-year period, but it would be subject to a harmonization of sectoral policies, a process which will prove difficult in practice.

The draft agreement also includes provisions on technical and phyto-zoosanitary barriers, unfair trade practices, intellectual property, governmental procurement, special safeguard procedures, services (particularly financial services, telecommunications, and transportation), foreign direct investment, and rules of origin. Provisions in some of these areas—particularly intellectual property and services—are less ambitious than Mexico expected at the onset of the final negotiation process in December 1993.

B. Chile

As negotiations with Mexico faced difficulties, Colombia and Venezuela signed bilateral free-trade agreements with Chile. Given the strong complementarity of the Chilean economy with those of Colombia and Venezuela, negotiations proved easy and were subject to no major opposition by their respective private sectors. Indeed, with respect to negotiations between Chile and Colombia, opposition was mainly led by Chilean textile producers. The Chilean-Venezuelan agreement was signed in April 1993; the Chilean-Colombian accord was signed in November 1993 and became effective in January 1994.

According to the current agreement, Colombia and Chile will liberalize their reciprocal trade at a fairly rapid pace, with few exceptions. The agreement includes four groups of goods: (1) those already covered by previous LAIA agreements (some agricultural goods, chemicals, and copper), for which tariffs were brought down to zero at the outset of the liberalization process; (2) a list of goods covering 90 percent of current trade, will be subject to a fairly rapid, three-year liberalization process; (3) a list of sensitive goods, such as oils and fats, copper manufactures, and most textiles, for which liberalization will take place in a five-year period; and (4) a list of exceptions, including sensitive agricultural products for Colombia and some textiles for Chile.

C. Central America and Caricom

Colombia and Venezuela have also been negotiating a free-trade agreement with members of the Central American Common Market (Costa Rica, El Salvador, Guatemala, Honduras, and Nicaragua). Although the intention to do so was expressed before and some contacts had been made, the current negotiation process was triggered by a presidential summit of the Group of Three and the Central American countries in Caracas in February 1993. The original expectation that a treaty would be signed by year's end was not fulfilled. In fact, the pace of negotiations was rather slow. Changes in the governments of several Central American countries, as well as of Venezuela and, later in the year, Colombia, may further slow negotiations in 1994.

Following LAIA principles, it has been agreed that there will be elements of nonreciprocity during the transition process. However, the specific way in which this principle will be applied has been subject to controversy. It has been agreed that the pace of the tariff cut will be faster for Colombia and Venezuela for each list of goods, classified according to their sensitivity to the countries involved. As in the case of the Group of Three, the design of the lists has proved difficult. This problem has been made more complex by the request by Central America that nonreciprocity be reflected in the design of the lists, in such a way that some goods could be classified as more sensitive to them than for Colombia and Venezuela. In practice this will mean that any goods classified by Central America in the exception list will be subject to a unilateral tariff cut by the South American countries, either temporarily or permanently. The controversy has been especially difficult with respect to agriculture. Central American countries have a particular interest in expanding the markets for such goods, but further liberalization of the sector has become a sensitive political issue in Colombia and Venezuela.

The issue of nonreciprocity has been even more troublesome in preliminary negotiations with the Caribbean Common Market (Caricom). In fact, Caricom members responded to the request by Colombia and Venezuela to negotiate a free-trade agreement by asking for a unilateral tariff cut by the South American countries. Such a petition is particularly difficult to deal with because many of the Caribbean islands have higher per-capita incomes than Colombia and even Venezuela. Thus, negotiations have not gone very far.

V. CONCLUSIONS

The consolidation of the Andean Group and the new free-trade agreements with other Latin American countries have been one of the priorities of economic reforms recently implemented in Colombia. Economic authorities clearly regard integration efforts as essential elements of trade liberalization measures to open markets to Colombian exports and, moreover, as steps towards a final objective of building a continental bloc of integration. The priority in this process has been integration with Venezuela, the major Latin American trading partner. The two countries have, in fact, built up a virtual customs union—a step which has proved difficult to implement in the Andean Group as a whole—and have jointly managed most negotiations with third countries. Colombia and Venezuela can, thus, be considered leaders of the continental integration process.

This process is not free of obstacles and uncertainties. Although a free-trade zone is in place among four of the five Andean countries, difficulties in negotiating the common external tariff, and political and economic difficulties faced at different times by Ecuador, Peru and, more recently, Venezuela have slowed the pace of consolidating the Andean Group. Moreover, despite the recent boom in intraregional trade, the integration coefficients of the Group are still low—a source, no doubt, of additional fragility. Uncertainties remain in the formation of the Group of Three and, much more, in the drafting of free-trade agreements with Central

America and Caricom. Only negotiations with Chile proved rather easy.

Even more difficult is the issue of eventual negotiations to join NAFTA and/or Mercosur. Currently, there are no evaluations of the benefits and costs of such decisions, nor has Colombia taken specific steps in either direction (except initial bilateral negotiations with some Mercosur members). It is in a privileged position with respect to NAFTA because the Andean Trade Preference Act (ATPA) gives Colombia ten-year preferential access on similar terms to the Caribbean Basin Initiative. As a result, 87 percent of Colombian nonoil exports currently enter the U.S. market free of tariffs. There is, moreover, a significant scope for export diversification within ATPA. However, it excludes certain important goods (in particular, textiles, apparel, footwear, sugar, and tuna fish), does not deal with sensitive nontariff barrier issues, and is subject to unilateral decisions by the United States. Distortions generated by the intersection between NAFTA and the Group of Three should also be a matter of concern. However, the net costs and benefits of NAFTA membership are not a subject of this paper.

NOTES

1. See, for example, Luis Jorge Garay, *El Pacto Andino, ¿Creación de un mercado para Colombia?* (Bogotá: Fedesarrollo, 1981).

2. In 1987, it was agreed that each country will be in charge of its direct foreign investment policy. On that basis, all have adopted fairly open investment regimes. In 1991, it was agreed that foreign firms could fully benefit from trade liberalization (restricted until then to those which signed commitments to become "mixed" or "domestic" firms). Finally, since 1991, the intellectual property regime has been significantly liberalized.

3. Fifty items of tariff schedule for Colombia, Peru, and Venezuela and 100 for Bolivia and Ecuador.

4. They related to differences in the system of variable levies (price bands), preferences granted by Venezuela to other Latin American countries in the Latin American Integration Association (LAIA), and the lack of harmonization of export promotion mechanisms, which allows Andean countries to exempt from import tariffs inputs used to produce goods exported to other Andean countries. Variable levies will be discussed later in the chapter.

5. Although political factors were invoked as the main reasons for this action, economic factors were also behind Peru's decision to suspend its obligations. As it will become clear in the following section, Peru's trade balance with the rest of the Andean Group had turned into an increasing deficit as a consequence of the overvaluation of its currency.

6. For a more extensive analysis of these developments, see Junta del Acuerdo de Cartagena, *Análisis del comercio andino, 1969–1980: evolución y características*, Lima, July 1982, and Pilar Esguerra, "El papel de las ventajas comparativas en el comercio andino de manufacturas," *Coyuntura Económica* (June 1986).

7. These estimates have been taken from José Antonio Ocampo and Leonardo Villar, "Fuentes de competitividad de las exportaciones industriales de Colombia," *Coyuntura Económica* (December 1993).

CENTRAL AMERICA:
Common Market, Trade Liberalization, and Trade Agreements

Ennio Rodríguez

This paper addresses three interrelated sets of issues: (1) the rationale for relaunching the Central American Common Market (CACM), initially created in 1960; (2) the new external environment created by the North American Free Trade Agreement (NAFTA); and (3) the tensions arising from the simultaneous and overlapping free-trade zone negotiations CACM countries are currently undertaking.

The peace process in the region, aimed at disentangling Central America from international geopolitics, relaunched regional integration for political and economic purposes. The relaunching of the CACM, as part of a peace and democratization process has included a change in some of the key features of the traditional economic development model based on import substitution. Third markets now have greater importance than in the past. These changes have created tensions since they alter the common set of rules that previously defined a common market.

The U.S. Caribbean Basin Initiative (CBI), enacted in 1985, granted preferential access to the U.S. market and has been very important for export diversification and investment attraction. However, the possibility of Mexico joining NAFTA has already affected investment decisions in the region and may have a serious impact on current exports.

Since 1990 Central American countries are negotiating free-trade zones with the United States within the Enterprise for the Americas Initiative (EAI). Mexico and Venezuela have also pro-

146

posed free-trade zones, motivated by the large trade surplus both countries enjoy with CACM, mainly as a result of supplying oil to the region and offering generous financing conditions. The European Community has also proposed trade negotiations. The issue of simultaneous and overlapping free-trade zones, and the tensions between bilateral and multilateral approaches to negotiations, may end up undermining the attempts to relaunch the CACM. Crucial components of the CACM, such as the common external tariff, rules of origin, dispute settlement mechanisms, and intellectual property rights may be changed in the attempts to negotiate free-trade zones. Consequently, the CACM may be reduced to another free-trade zone.

Prior to addressing these issues, brief antecedents need to be mentioned. First, the five countries of Central America[1] always have had open economies. On average, these countries are more open (60.3 percent) than both Mexico (37.1 percent) and Chile (55.0 percent), as measured by the trade/gross domestic product (GDP) ratio in 1989. There are, however, important deviations from this average: Costa Rica is the most open economy of the region (90.6 percent) and Guatemala the most closed (44.4 percent) (see Table 6.1). Trade policy options are clearly limited by this fact, which is, to some extent, the unavoidable result of the smallness of these economies. The costs of closing an economy are higher the smaller the economy is, given that the efficiency losses can be expected to be larger.

Second, the United States is the single most important trading partner for Central America. The share of exports to the United States has increased significantly, from 34.7 percent in 1970 to 40.2 percent in 1990. This contrasts sharply with the decline in intra-CACM exports, which fell from 26.1 percent to 14.4 percent during the same period (see Table 6.2).

Third, Central America already has preferential access to the U.S. market as a result of unilateral trade concessions granted under the CBI and enhanced CBI II (1991) agreements. Although CBI contained important exceptions (textiles, footwear, sugar, and other tropical products), it effectively put the region on the investor's map. The overall impact has been positive, but because internal political conditions and the degree of economic reform vary by country, the benefits have been unevenly distributed in the region.

Table 6.1

Degree of Openness of Central American and Other Selected
Countries and Groups of Countries, 1989.

Country/Group	Imports/GDP (%)	Exports/GDP (%)	Trade/GDP (%)
Costa Rica	43.8	46.8	90.6
El Salvador	32.1	24.9	57.0
Guatemala	22.5	21.9	44.4
Honduras	32.9	34.2	67.1
Nicaragua	37.9	17.3	55.3
CACM[a]	31.3	28.9	60.3
Chile	24.6	30.4	55.0
Mexico	14.4	22.8	37.1
ALADI[a]	11.7	20.6	32.3
United States	11.1	9.5	20.6
Group of Seven[a]	16.5	16.6	33.1
EEC[a]	28.5	29.4	58.0

[a]Weighted averages.

ALADI = Latin American Integration Association

EEC = European Economic Community

Source: CEPAL, "La coordinación de las políticas macroeconómicas en el contexto de la integración centroamericana," LC/L.630 (1991a).

CBI II provided an indefinite extension and important improvements, such as exemption from the cumulative clause. This exemption means that the United States will not add exports from CBI countries to those from other countries when determining injury to U.S. producers. As a result, 80 percent of Costa Rican products entering the United States (those that pay no tariffs) are less likely to continue suffering from countervailing duties.

CBI is a unilateral trade concession by the United States. Thus, tariff preferences are non-contractual; the United States can unilaterally remove a country from beneficiary status and/or re-

Table 6.2
Central America Exports by Destination (1970–1990)

Destination	1970	1980 (percent)	1985	1990[a]
United States	34.7	35.2	42.5	40.2
Central American Common Market	26.1	25.5	13.7	14.4
European Economic Community		24.9[b]	23.8	22.1
Mexico	0.3	0.8	0.7	1.4
Other	38.9	13.6	19.3	21.9
Total	100.0	100.0	100.0	100.0

[a]Preliminary
[b]1981
Source: CEPAL based on IMF, Direction of Trade Statistics, DOTS.

move a product from CBI eligibility for all or for individual countries.

Fourth, however, the privileged trade access to U.S. markets has eroded since the enactment of CBI II. The United States has granted similar trade concessions to the Andean Pact countries in exchange for anti-drug production efforts. The negotiations of the NAFTA are another source of erosion.

Fifth, Central America has undertaken a process of trade liberalization with regards to third markets and in the context of relaunching the CACM. Countries have reduced state intervention in the economy, allowing market forces a greater role in allocating resources. They have cut tariffs significantly. Prior to the first reform, average legal tariffs were lowest in Honduras (41 percent) and highest in Nicaragua (54 percent). By 1987 tariff rates had been cut nearly by half: Honduras had the lowest (20 percent) and Costa Rica the highest (26 percent). In the July 1991 summit in San Salvador, the presidents agreed on further reductions and a common external tariff (5 percent minimum and 20 percent maximum to be achieved by 1993) (see Table 6.3).

These efforts at trade liberalization, in concert with the enactment of CBI, resulted in increased concentration of exports in

Table 6.3
Legal Tariffs in Central America (percentages)

	Average tariff prior to reform[a]	Average tariff 1987	Range 1991	Range 1993
Costa Rica	52	26[b]	20–70[c]	5–20
El Salvador	48	23	5–35	5–20
Guatemala	50	25	5–40[d]	5–20
Honduras	41	20	9–50[e]	5–20
Nicaragua	54	21	5–95[f]	5–20

[a]Equivalent *ad valorem* average tariff prior to the tariff reform.

[b]Includes surcharges.

[c]Includes a 10 percent surcharge on extraregional imports. A deposit of 30 percent of the CIF value of imports was also required by the Central Bank.

[d]Includes a 3 percent surcharge on extraregional imports.

[e]Includes a general surcharge of 5 percent and an additional 10 percent on final goods.

[f]Includes selective consumption taxes up to 75 percent (equivalent to tariffs).

Sources: CEPAL, "Políticas industriales en Centroamérica y Panamá," LC/MEX/R.310 (1991); World Bank, "Trade Liberalization and Economic Integration in Central America," Report no. 7625-CAM (1990); Tenth Presidential Summit, San Salvador, 1991.

the U.S. market, giving more prominence to issues of access to the U.S. market.[2] The EAI proposes a framework for increased trade and introduces the element of reciprocity, which was absent from previous unilateral trade concessions granted by the United States.

Sixth, both Mexico and Venezuela have proposed trade liberalization initiatives to the CACM. These proposals recognize the asymmetry in the levels of development among the countries, but they make provision for eventual reciprocity.

In short, Central America is faced with multiple trade negotiations and has undertaken unilateral trade liberalization. Multiple negotiations raise a set of issues regarding potential tradeoffs and administrative conundrums. Furthermore, the meaning and potential of the CACM in the context of unilateral liberalizations and possible bilateral and/or multilateral trade concessions becomes a critical issue to be addressed in this paper.

RELAUNCHING THE CACM AND THE EROSION OF CBI
PREFERENCES

Relaunching the CACM

The well-known rupture of the CACM during the 1980s was not triggered by the unilateral processes of trade liberalization. A deep-rooted political and military crisis, with wide international support to antagonistic forces, coincided with an exhaustion of the potential of import-substituting industrialization and a decline in traditional export commodities. The crisis erupted in international trade as defaulted payments started to accumulate within the CACM.[3]

In the midst of this crisis, the first processes of unilateral trade liberalization started. For a variety of ideological and geopolitical reasons, international organizations and groups in the region began to debate the usefulness of the CACM.

Trade liberalizations generated tensions among the CACM partners, particularly in tariff and exchange-rate policies. Policy differences resulted from varying degrees of acceptance of the need for stabilization and structural adjustment, as well as of the speed of the changes required to achieve results. Eventually, however, an increasing homogeneity in philosophical views and in economic policy orientations of the presidents of the region eroded the initial differences. Trade liberalization and third market export promotion became shared objectives, and economic integration assumed a new role.[4]

Peace-making initiatives in the region relaunched regional integration for political and economic purposes. The emerging consensus on trade liberalization vis-à-vis third markets and on macroeconomic policies made possible new agreements on external tariffs (see Table 6.3) and indicated the willingness of countries to coordinate macroeconomic policies.

Political will for economic integration has repeatedly been expressed in the periodic summits of presidents and meetings of vice-presidents, chancellors, economic cabinets, and other ministerial-level reunions. Declarations and agreements have occurred at a rate that may surpass regional implementation capabilities, but they express a strong political determination to relaunch Central American integration.[5] These new efforts have found increasing support from multilateral organizations and the United States, which are changing their policies to favor common markets and free-trade zones. This is particularly true since the United States launched the EAI in June 1990.

The regional peace plan that emerged from the Esquipulas II presidential summit on August 6–7, 1987 set the political precedent for revitalizing economic integration. The electoral defeat of the Sandinistas in 1989 created additional room for wider political consensus. At the Antigua summit (June 17, 1990), economic issues began to dominate the agenda, and the "Plan of Economic Action for Central America" (PAECA) was developed. The plan views regional economic integration as a foundation for a joint, outward-looking strategy.[6]

The president of Panama attended the Antigua summit as an observer and later joined as a full participant in the July 1991 summit in San Salvador. In a subsequent summit in Tegucigalpa, the prime minister of Belize participated as an observer. Evidently political developments continued to precede economic events. Flanking Central America to the south and north, Panama and Belize would seem natural extensions of the CACM.[7]

At the tenth summit in July 1991, an agreement was reached on a new common external tariff by 1993. A common external tariff had been established at the initiation of the CACM, and remained in effect until 1986, but after Honduras withdrew from the CACM in 1970,[8] only the four remaining members observed it. Honduras remained an active trading partner via bilateral trade agreements that did not include a common external tariff. At the San Salvador summit, the Honduran president announced that the bilateral agreements were to become multilateral. This restored some normality to the CACM.

The institutional development of the CACM is particularly rich.[9] The Central American Economic Integration Secretariat and the Central American Bank for Economic Integration have been key institutions. Both suffered severely from the crisis of the 1980s but have undergone significant processes of modernization. The bank in particular has improved its financial situation.

The contraction of intraregional trade during the crisis was severe. The value of total exports declined from 1.1 billion Central American pesos[10] in 1980 to 0.4 billion in 1986. As intraregional trade declined, an intraregional import substitution—with the resulting efficiency losses—took place. Simultaneously, third market exports increased their share in total exports, from 15.7 percent in 1980 to 22.3 percent in 1986. Since 1987, intraregional trade has experienced a sustained recovery, but the peak levels of 1980 have yet to be reached.

An interesting new development of economic integration has been the strengthening of private-sector regional organizations and the appearance of new ones.[11] This is a promising development that reflects common interests and creates regional lobbying groups.

The new aim of economic integration is to promote regional international competitiveness, replacing import-substituting industrialization. Consequently, greater emphasis will be given to third markets and to sectors such as financial services and agriculture.[12] Intraregional trade is likely to grow slowly as extraregional imports and exports expand. New mechanisms of integration such as capital markets, regional transnational investment projects and joint trade negotiation in the General Agreement on Trade and Tariffs (GATT), and other trade initiatives may provide new grounds for regional cooperation. These may be less disruptive than the previous competing commercial interests.

To the extent that the countries see themselves in competition with each other, third market export development may be a centrifugal force. Attempts to complement supply among countries and to enter joint negotiations may, however, counteract such force. The same effect may be expected from the tendency of international investors and buyers to see the region as a whole and as competing with other regions.[13]

Two critical issues that may undermine the new regional integrationist efforts are the distribution of costs and benefits of intraregional trade liberalization among trading partners, and the negotiation of wider free-trade zones with relatively larger and more developed partners. A third issue on which the success of the strategy of export promotion to third markets *cum* regional integration has depended has been the preferential access to U.S. market as a result of CBI.

Experience suggests that unequal distribution of costs and benefits can be very disruptive. In the previous design of the CACM, the uneven levels of development were counteracted with slower paces of trade liberalization, credit programs, and planned distribution of industries. The latter was never implemented as regional industrial policy never got off the ground, and the other two instruments failed to significantly offset the greater costs incurred by Honduras.

In relaunching the CACM no new mechanisms of cost compensation have been considered. The absence of a regional or community budget precludes allocating compensatory expenditures to the less-developed countries or regions, as is done in the European Community. Capital and investment flows may play a greater compensating role than in the past, as cheaper labor or natural resources may be available on a regional basis. The fact remains, however, that the uneven distribution of benefits and costs may be a future disruptive force.

NAFTA and the Erosion of CBI Preferences

As previously mentioned, Central American preferential access to the U.S. market has been very important for export diversification and investment attraction. However, the possibility of Mexico joining NAFTA has begun to affect investment decisions in the region[14] and may have a serious impact on current exports. According to the estimates of the organized private sector of Central America,[15] CBI enjoys preferential access over Mexico on 7 percent of CBI imports into the United States. The remaining 93 percent of CBI imports into the United States today enjoy no preferences over Mexican exports (see Table 6.4).

NAFTA's provisions could put 60 percent of CBI exports to the United States at a disadvantage in terms of the level of tariffs and non-tariff barriers (NTBs) with Mexican exports. First are the 15 percent of CBI exports that enter the United States under CBI or the Generalized System of Preferences (GSP) and are in the GSP list. United States authorities have indicated their intention to bind duties immediately on Mexican GSP products at a zero rate. Second are the 45 percent Most Favored Nation (MFN) exports of sensitive products. United States authorities have indicated that NAFTA concessions on these products will be introduced slowly but will start immediately and increase progressively.

Mexico may become a most attractive production site for this 60 percent of CBI exports for two reasons. First, concessions to Mexico will be made on a contractual free-trade agreement (FTA),

Table 6.4
CBI Imports by Import Program, 1990

	Billion US$	Percent
Imports subject to zero duty under Most Favored Nation (MFN)	2.5	33
MFN dutiable imports eligible for the Generalized System of Preferences (GSP) and CBI	1.1	15
MFN dutiable imports eligible for CBI but not GSP	0.5	7
MFN dutiable imports not eligible for CBI or GSP	3.4	45
TOTAL	7.5	100

Source: FEDEPRICAP, based on the *Sixth Annual Report on the Impact of the Caribbean Basin Recovery Act on U.S. Industries and Consumers* (1991).

which is more secure than the unilateral CBI concessions. Second, investors will know the net result of the process of increasing concessions from the outset and will act accordingly.

Although CBI put Central America on the map for U.S. investors, the consequences of Mexico joining NAFTA have been far greater, overshadowing CBI. The attention and enthusiasm about Mexico's economic reforms, its close proximity to the United States, its considerable market, and the prospect of an FTA make it very difficult for Central America to compete as an attractive investment site. The complex political situation emerging from a decade of war and social strife is such that the region cannot risk reducing growth rates. This makes the possible investment and trade diversion effects of NAFTA a special concern for the region.

This analysis clearly shows that increasing, guaranteed market access to the United States is critical for Central America. Such access would include, on the basis of NAFTA: 1) moving from the unilateral trade concessions of CBI to a contractual format; and 2) increasing market access on par with that to be obtained by Mexico, and preferably, with increased access in particular sectors such as textiles and apparel, leather, and agricultural and tropical products.

The argument that Central America will benefit as a result of growth within NAFTA underestimates the potential effects of trade and investment diversion. Some analysts have suggested that, since Mexico is expected to benefit most from NAFTA, Central America should increase its trade links with Mexico. As Table 6.2 demonstrates, however, current exports from the region to Mexico are only 1.4 percent of total exports. Even dramatic growth rates of such exports are not likely to have a large impact. In contrast, 40.2 percent of current exports from Central America go to the United States, making it the region's single largest market. More-over, most nontraditional exports from Central America are destined for the U.S. market. Expected growth in exports from Central America to the United States, spurred by NAFTA, may in fact be offset by the loss of actual and potential market share to Mexico. Thus, ongoing competitive access to the U.S. market is critical to the region's economic recovery.

FEDEPRICAP has proposed four options for the CBI bene-ficiaries to gain improved market access to the United States within the same time frame of negotiation and implementation of NAFTA:[16]

(1) Negotiate a regional FTA, which would supplement CBI, to provide concessions similar to NAFTA's in exchange for market-opening concessions from CBI. A fast-track approval of the legislation[17] may be necessary for con-cessions on sensitive products. CBI concessions would not be enough for a full-fledged FTA, but would be sufficiently attractive to the U.S. business community to gain its support for the arrangement. The arrangement would be temporary, aimed at maintaining pressure for economic reform leading to a full-fledged FTA, or incor-poration into NAFTA.

(2) Pursue improvements to the CBI through legislation. The pending CBI III bill could be expanded to bring in the benefits included in NAFTA, and, in particular, making the concessions contractual.

(3) Negotiate CBI improvements (making them contractual and improving access for specific CBI imports) in the Uruguay Round of GATT or on the fringes of the Round for inclusion in the implementing legislation.

(4) Provide special status for CBI within NAFTA. Interim solutions could include providing associate status with

full benefits but only partial obligations and treating CBI products as NAFTA products in establishing origin.

This specific mechanism illustrates that if the political will exists, policymakers can find a way to avoid further deterioration of the CBI investment climate. However, the response of the U.S. Trade Representative (USTR) to FEDEPRICAP proposals was cautious; the USTR suggested the enactment of satisfactory intellectual property rights and the negotiation of bilateral investment treaties while Central America proceeded with economic reforms.[18]

On March 18, 1993, U.S. Congressman Samuel Gibbons introduced a proposal titled "Caribbean Basin Free-Trade Agreement Act," which would extend fast-track negotiating authority until mid-1996. The authority would be for negotiating the access of CBI countries to NAFTA, with adequate supplementary or reciprocal commercial agreements similar to NAFTA. This proposal also addresses the potential impact of NAFTA on CBI exports of textiles, apparel, and sugar.

The Gibbons proposal is in the early stages of the legislative process, and there is no certainty that it will be approved. Previous attempts by Gibbons and others to benefit the CBI region have been unsuccessful, and for its part, the Senate has opposed attempts to improve CBI legislation. Even if approved, this legislation would only be an invitation to the executive to negotiate. The U.S. administration would then have to initiate negotiations with individual countries or groups of countries from the region.

It must be mentioned that despite the unilateral concessions granted under CBI, no evidence exists to show a resulting adverse impact on U.S. industry. In fact, 1990 was the fourth consecutive year in which the United States registered record exports ($9.3 billion) to CBI beneficiaries and a trade surplus of $1.8 billion.

EXTRAREGIONAL NEGOTIATIONS

Extraregional Free-Trade Zones

Central America is negotiating a free-trade zone with the United States within the EAI. Mexico and Venezuela have also proposed free-trade zones with Central America, motivated by the large trade surplus both countries enjoy with CACM, mainly as a result of supplying oil to the region and offering generous financing. The European Community has also proposed trade negotiations. Before addressing the issues of simultaneous and overlapping free-trade zones we will examine their relative potential and importance.

Potential benefits and costs from a free-trade zone. Traditional evaluations of a free-trade zone distinguish between static and dynamic effects.

Static effects. Frequently a great deal of time and effort is spent analyzing the static effects.[19] To achieve less distorted production and consumption, trade diversion (displacing the third market's more efficient suppliers by the trading partner) is the negative effect, and trade creation (displacement of less efficient local suppliers by the trading partner) is the positive effect. Trade theory argues that benefits outweigh costs to the extent that trade creation exceeds trade diversion.

Trade creation will be greater depending upon: (1) the level of the tariff or NTBs before the free-trade zone is established; (2) the volume of exports; (3) the extent to which lower tariffs are translated into lower domestic prices; (4) the price elasticity of demand for imports; and (5) the elasticity of export supply.[20] As a result, the magnitude of the effects of trade creation depends both on the current features of trade flows and structures and on the characteristics of the FTA, in particular, the reduction achieved in tariffs and NTBs for relevant categories for the trading partners.

Trade diversion will depend on factors (1) to (3), plus two more: (4) the elasticity of substitution between the trading partners' products and third country products; and, (5) the volume of imports from the rest of the world.

The analysis of trade diversion and trade creation, particularly given the values assumed for the aforementioned variables for Central America and the United States, leads to the conclusion that import penetration will be higher for Central America. Consequently, the adjustment costs will be higher and the region will enjoy a greater increase in consumer welfare (net of adjustment costs). It may also be concluded that, in terms of static effects, the trade balance for Central America will deteriorate. At the same time, however, to the extent that the high concentration of exports in U.S. markets will mean a greater potential for export growth, the incentive to negotiate an FTA will increase. This result has to be qualified by the fact that Central America already enjoys tariff-free access on a wide range of products. But there are important exceptions (sugar, textiles and apparel, and leather) which, if included, would have important growth potential.

In contrast, there is less incentive to negotiate FTAs with Mexico and Venezuela because export growth potential to both markets can be expected to have a low impact on global Central American exports. Central America already enjoys preferential access to some Mexican states with little impact on trade flows. In the case of Mexico, the values assumed by the analysis of static effects suggest that import penetration will be greater for the region. Consequently, increases in consumer welfare will also be greater, but further deterioration of the trade balance for Central America is also to be expected. With Venezuela the results are more uncertain.

The European Community is the region's second-largest trading partner and therefore market access is critical, particularly for sensitive products such as bananas. Recently CACM countries have faced a potential upsurge of protection as Economic Community countries announced quotas and tariffs for this second most important product of the region. An FTA would be of great interest to Central America if it would ensure access for existing and potential exports such as agricultural products, textiles, and apparel, which currently are heavily protected. Import penetration would be higher for the CACM, assuming that liberalization would include a wide range of goods.

Although rigorous results can be presented using a static-effects approach, in reality they may not be relevant. First, trade diversion may not necessarily lead to a loss in efficiency (welfare) in cases where, although the new supplier may be less efficient, the duty-free price paid by producers and consumers may be lower than previously. Second, empirical estimates indicate that static costs and benefits tend to be modest.[21] In short, greater emphasis should be placed on the less neat but more important dynamic effects.[22]

Dynamic effects. An FTA could affect the rate of growth of the trading partners as a result of (1) the scale economies achieved on the basis of increased market size; (2) external economies; (3) polarization effects (in absolute or real terms) on regions or between trading partners, resulting from the adjustment costs of trade creation in one region or country and/or the concentration of investment in another region or country; and (4) the efficiency of production and investment due to enhanced competition and an improved macroeconomic environment.[23] Although analytically appealing, these factors do not easily lead to an a priori analysis of the impact of an FTA. It can be expected, however, that factors (1), (2), and (4) will have a negligible or positive effect on all trading partners. It is factor (3), polarization effects, that is of concern. Adjustment costs can be very high for less-developed economies. These could be counteracted by the patterns of investment and by the transitional measures agreed upon, such as the timing of tariff reduction. The current investment climate in Central America would appear as a critical factor both for reducing adjustment costs and for benefiting from the trade potential. Clearly, the negotiating process is important to define transitional measures that recognize the existing asymmetry between trading partners and the risk of polarization. This is true of all four FTAs described in the static-effects analysis. If they were to occur simultaneously, the compounded effect on Central America could be devastating unless adequate transitional considerations were included.

Characteristics of the free-trade zone emerging from the EAI. From an analytical point of view, the larger the free-trade zone, the greater the benefits and the lower the potential losses from trade diversion. The EAI calls for a free-trade area from Anchorage to Cape Horn, but it could be designed according to two extremes or any combination in between. The extremes would be: a) a multilateral free-trade agreement in which all borders in the continent would be lifted for trade purposes, and b) a set of bilateral free-trade agreements resulting in what Wonnacot has called a hub-and-spoke system, "in which the United States, as the hub in a rimless wheel, has a bilateral spoke agreement with each of the other countries. While the United States would be trading freely with each spoke country, none of the spoke countries would be trading freely with any of the others."[24]

If the signed framework agreements among the United States and potential EAI participants are an indication of the final outcome of what the actual trading system would look like, it would be a combination of the aforementioned extremes. It essentially would be a hub-and-spoke system, but some of the spokes would be of considerable size and would involve a multilateral free-trade zone (such as NAFTA, Caricom, and Mercosur) while others would be typical spokes, such as the Central American countries seem to prefer.[25]

From an analytical perspective, a multilateral free-trade system is clearly preferable to a set of bilateral trade treaties. But countries that are first to enter free-trade agreements may prefer a hub-and-spoke system. Since trade and investment diversion may create growth that is detrimental to third parties, first comers will have a competitive edge in market share—an advantage that may prevail in view of the initial difficulties of latecomers.

The United States could have considerable weight in promoting a multilateral free-trade zone, but there are strong incentives for the United States to seek bilateral treaties. First, there is the need to achieve results; the complexities of a multilateral free-trade zone may be insurmountable, according to political calendars. Second, if countries are ready (in terms of economic reforms and political will) to sign an FTA, why should the United States make them wait for the slow movers and sacrifice the growth potential to be derived precisely from moving fast? In the case of Central America, however, a regional approach is preferable. The CACM provides a unified administrative structure for negotiating and would work to preserve the benefits of the customs union.

CACM and Multiple Trade Negotiations

The CACM partners are GATT members[26] and have thereby accepted multilateral norms for trade. They are engaged in negotiations with the United States, Mexico, and Venezuela, and in a revision of the Luxembourg Accord with the European Community. Despite being consistent with GATT, these negotiations may create tensions and/or openly contradict some of the fundamentals of the CACM. In terms of the wider view of using Central American integration as the basis for third market exports, negotiating additional free-trade zones seems a sensible strategy to secure market access and increase domestic efficiency. Problems arise, however, in the combination of multilateral and bilateral approaches and the possibly inconsistent definitions of numerous matters, including tariffs, rules of origin, dumping, and dispute settlements.[27]

Tariffs. In August 1991 the CACM countries reached an agreement on external tariffs and related issues such as unfair trade. They set the maximum tariff at 20 percent, the minimum at 5 percent, with two intermediate tariffs of 10 and 15 percent. The agreement needs to be ratified by the five congresses.[28]

Negotiations with the United States under the EAI have advanced to the point of signing framework agreements. An important departure of the framework agreements from the CBI is the element of reciprocity and the inclusion of new areas for negotiation, namely investments, services, and intellectual property rights. Central American countries chose to sign bilateral agreements in contrast with Caricom and Mercosur. Since the bilateral negotiations have not addressed issues such as tariffs, rules of origin, and unfair trade practices, they have been compatible with the rulings of the CACM. The potential for conflict emerges, however, if the countries continue to negotiate individually, and if a mechanism for resolving possible contradictions is not defined. If some countries are prepared to move faster and the United States is willing to accept bilateral negotiations, such actions would eliminate the common external tariff and could undermine other CACM elements such as intellectual property rights, rules of origin, and dispute settlements.

The time frame for these negotiations is expected to be rather long, and as access to U.S. markets is critical for the CACM economies, the transitory measures suggested above become very relevant. The United States has clearly indicated that it will not negotiate any further free-trade agreements until Mexico joins NAFTA. The Congress may want to evaluate the results of Mexico joining NAFTA before initiating additional FTAs, entailing further delays. Since Chile is in line as the second likely FTA candidate, there will no doubt be considerable delay in implementing the EAI even under the most optimistic assumptions.

Central American countries have already begun to implement the type of reforms that the EAI signaled as preconditions for participation. However, according to USTR officials, the progress is still not sufficient to warrant an interim FTA.[29] It is not clear that this opinion is based on actual evaluation of current economic reforms in Central America, or whether it reflects a changed political climate in the United States in which Central America no longer enjoys preferential attention. Some U.S. policymakers may believe that Central America has benefited sufficiently from the CBI I and II trade agreements. The USTR officials also expressed that Central America would benefit indirectly as a result of growth sparked by NAFTA, which would increase demand for Central American products. They concluded that it would be important for Central America to strengthen economic relations with Mexico to take greater advantage of growth to be generated.[30]

A comparison between CBI concessions and NAFTA is particularly relevant. Some concessions are being eroded as privileged access is extended to Mexico. If Mexico obtains improved access, some concessions may also be downgraded. Others may be threatened if CBI concessions are removed unilaterally as a consequence of the process to approve NAFTA, which may involve attempts to harmonize concessions.

Textiles are the area of major concern. They are excluded from duty-free treatment under CBI and are subject to import restraints under the Multifiber Agreement.[31] NAFTA provides for immediate quota elimination and tariff phase-out for qualifying Mexican exports of textiles and apparel.[32] Other sectors excluded from CBI, and in which Mexico will eventually have an advantage, include sugar, footwear, and leather.

Negotiations between the CACM partners and Mexico started with the Summit of Tuxtla Gutiérrez, where participants stated the will to create a free-trade zone by December 1996. It presupposes reciprocity on concessions but recognizes the asymmetrical levels of development. In August 1992 a multilateral framework agreement was signed that defines the parameters for bilateral negotiations on certain subjects while leaving other matters to be treated bilaterally.

The list of products subject to free trade and the conditions and time frame for tariff reduction are to be negotiated bilaterally. If the bilateral approach is pursued and the common external tariff is maintained, the only goods available for consideration in a free-trade zone with Mexico would be those not included in the CACM. A second alternative would be for all CACM countries to accept what was negotiated by the first country. A third approach would be a process of consultation and harmonization equivalent to a multilateral agreement.

Accepting different lists of products and/or tariffs would introduce distortions in the effective levels of protection harmonized by the common external tariff and would reduce the benefits of a customs union. There would also be grounds for accusations of unfair trade among CACM partners and incentives for contraband trade.[33]

At a July 16, 1991 summit, the presidents of the CACM and Venezuela signed the Basis for an Agreement on Trade and Investment. In September 1992 Venezuela presented a proposal for negotiations that included an asymmetrical and multilateral approach in which 23 percent of Central American exports to Venezuela would be granted immediate duty-free access. This percentage would increase annually, and the CACM would start opening to Venezuelan exports six years after the accord came into full force with the terms and conditions to be negotiated before December 1993.

The European Community has agreed with Central America to revise the Luxembourg Accord, but proposes strict reciprocity. There will be no preferential access for Central America, and no special recognition (as in the case of Andean countries) for relatively lower levels of development. The tariff aspect of the negotiation will thus be related to the most favored nation clause of the GATT. There is no reference to the generalized system of preferences. From the point of view of the CACM, the European Community's proposal is compatible with existing arrangements, but the stance, requiring reciprocity, is clearly a tougher one.

Rules of origin. An important aspect of the CACM is the definition of rules of origin, which were more rigorously defined in the Multilateral Treaty of July 1991. The importance of adequate rules of origin increases in the case of free-trade zones, which do not include common external tariffs, as the country with lowest tariffs could become the port of entry to the other partners. Countries involved in multiple free-trade zones, might accept a number of different rules of origin, making way for inefficiencies, distortions, and administrative complications, which could lead to corruption. For example, products from a relatively more developed partner, with which rules of origin are less strict than within the CACM, could give place to efficiency losses as regional production is substituted by the free-trade zone partner.

Negotiations with the United States have yet to reach the stage of defining rules of origin. It is one of the issues for which the multilateral approach is most sensible.

Rules of origin are more lenient within CBI than within NAFTA. The difference is mainly in third country content. NAFTA mandates that products not wholly produced in a NAFTA country must undergo a change in tariff classification to be eligible. In some cases, a minimum value added is required, either in addition to or instead of the transformation rule.[34] CBI requires products containing third country components to have at least 35 percent of their value resulting from processing in one or more CBI countries, and the products must have been substantially transformed into a new and different article. However, NAFTA has the *de minimis* rule, under which the non-NAFTA content is less than 7 percent to classify for duty-free treatment. There is no need for complex documentation nor proof of transformation. CBI has no *de minimis* rule.

In the free-trade zone with Mexico, the multilateral framework did not include rules of origin and these are therefore left for bilateral negotiations. In the case of Venezuela, rules of origin have not been agreed upon or even proposed yet. The Economic Community has proposed adopting compatible rulings.

Unfair trade and safeguards. The CACM has defined unfair trade, export subsidies, and safeguards. Different definitions in other free-trade zones could create distorted incentives and administrative complications. The difficulties would be further aggravated if CACM countries were to also accept bilateral definitions. Venezuela and the European Community have proposed GATT definitions and procedures for these matters; negotiations with the United States have yet to reach the point of discussing concrete proposals.

The CBI exempts the region from the cumulation clause for products under investigation in anti-dumping and countervailing duty cases from imports from non-beneficiaries also under investigation. Since CBI countries are rarely large suppliers, they usually are shielded from affirmative injury findings. Mexico enjoys no similar exemption under NAFTA.

The framework agreement between Mexico and the CACM contains definitions that, although basically similar to those

adopted by the CACM, could be subject to different interpreta-
tions, as in the case of safeguards. Safeguards can be triggered only
if imports cause actual serious injury to local production, whereas
GATT accepts safeguards when imports threaten to cause serious
injury. The acceptance of this more strict definition by the CACM
may protect Mexican imports vis-à-vis those from the rest of the
world. In the multilateral framework, safeguards are accepted for
a year, which can be extended; in the CACM, safeguards are
expected to last for a shorter span and be eliminated entirely after
one year.[35]

Dispute settlement. Mechanisms for bilateral dispute settlements can affect third parties.[36] This possibility is more likely to
materialize if bilateral mechanisms with a third party are accepted
by members of a common market. Central America has defined
a multilateral mechanism for dispute settlements within the
CACM. With the United States, the issue has not yet been addressed, and with Mexico and Venezuela it has been left for later
definition. The European Community has indicated preference for
GATT procedures.

NAFTA establishes a Trade Commission as a mechanism for
dispute settlement that hinders the U.S. government from acting
unilaterally. Under CBI, the United States can act unilaterally and
withdraw concessions.

CONCLUSIONS

1. Relaunching the CACM can be justified in terms of intraregional trade potential, pooling together of scarce bargaining
teams and resources, efficiency of investments, and other areas of
regional cooperation. Historical justifications also abound. Securing market access in third countries is a clear priority in the face of
the outward-looking development strategy pursued.

2. The objective of re-creating the CACM is incompatible
with bilateral trade negotiations if these are to be meaningful. It is
thus necessary for Central American countries to approach these
negotiations jointly. The evidence of the past two years suggests
some preference for bilateralism, as reflected in the bilateral framework agreements with the United States, and the Nicaraguan and

Costa Rican bilateral talks with Mexico. If the bilateral approach is chosen, it is likely that the CACM will become a free-trade zone.

3. Multiple free-trade zones can create administrative and incentive complications that should be carefully examined. In particular, since free-trade zones include reciprocity, careful consideration should be given to the likely impact on regional production and the type of asymmetry required. Also, multiple negotiations demand human and material resources simply not available in the region.

4. The consolidation of the CACM and the definition of strategies vis-à-vis third markets should take place before additional free-trade zones are negotiated. If not, the combination of bilateral pressures may totally undermine the regional effort. It is possible, however, that third parties could become agents of consolidation of a regional approach to trade negotiations and accept the objective of strengthening the CACM.

5. The United States heads the list in export concentration priorities for the CACM. However, since a free-trade zone is not in the near future, the CACM must negotiate effectively to prevent the erosion of CBI concessions. Negotiations with Mexico follow in terms of priority.

6. A comparison between CBI concessions and NAFTA is particularly relevant. In some cases CBI concessions are being eroded as the United States extends privileged access or provides improved access to Mexico. It is conceivable that attempts to harmonize concessions as part of the approval process of NAFTA may result in unilaterally removing CBI concessions. A top priority for the CACM countries is the defense of the CBI. In addition, some form of transitory extension of benefits obtained by Mexico is necessary if the investment dynamism generated by the initiative is to be sustained.

NOTES

1. Costa Rica, El Salvador, Guatemala, Honduras, and Nicaragua.

2. Prior to the Enterprise for the Americas Initiative a free-trade zone was proposed including Canada, the United States, Mexico, and CBI beneficiaries. See E. Rodríguez, P. A. Morales, M. Figueres, and S. Weisleder, "Análisis de las oportunidades de expansión brindadas por la Iniciativa de la Cuenca del Caribe," *Alternativas de Desarrollo,* prepared

for the Secretaría de Integración Económica de Centroamérica, August 1989. The organized private sector of Central America (FEDEPRICAP) later developed a detailed proposal and presented it to U.S. authorities. See S. Lande and C. Nellis, "Acuerdo de justo comercio entre norteamérica y mesoamérica. Un continente más competitivo en un ambiente global cambiante," in *Desafío del Desarrollo Centroamericano*, ed. Ennio Rodríguez (San José: EUNED, 1991).

3. This section is partially based on Ennio Rodríguez, "Mercado Común Centroamericano: Apertura e Integración," in *Los Procesos de Integración Económica en América Latina*, ed. R. Bouzas (Madrid: Fundación CEDEAL, 1993).

4. For a review of export promotion policies see CEPAL, "Políticas industriales en Centroamérica y Panamá," LC/MEX/R.314 (1991).

5. For a review of agreements and declarations of the summits and their monitoring see SIECA, "Contenido temático de los mandatos y declaraciones de las cumbres de presidentes de Centroamérica" (mimeo, 1991) and SIECA, "Informe del avance de los mandatos de las cumbres de presidentes de Centroamérica" (mimeo, 1991).

6. "Impulsar el desarrollo sostenido de Centroamérica mediante una estrategia conjunta hacia afuera, estableciendo mecanismos de consulta y coordinación para fortalecer la participación de nuestras economías en el comercio internacional," *Declaración de Antigua*, Antigua, June 17, 1990.

7. Although not without complications. Panama is open in the financial-services sector and highly protectionist in both agriculture and industry. Belize participates in Caribbean integrationist efforts and institutions and is also a Lômé country.

8. This resulted from the war with El Salvador and complaints about the uneven distribution of costs and benefits of economic integration.

9. For a chronological description of the Central American institutions, see CEPAL, "Perfil de la integración centroamericana," LC/MEX/R.341 (1992).

10. One U.S. dollar equals one peso.

11. These are: Federación de Cámaras de Exportadores de Centroamérica (FECAEXCA), Federación de Cámaras de Industria de Centroamérica (FECAICA), Federación de Cámaras de Comercio del Istmo Centroamericano (FECAMCA), Federación de Entidades Privadas de Centroamérica y Panamá (FEDEPRICAP), Instituto Centroamericano de Administración de Empresas (INCAE), and la Asociación de Usuarios del Transporte Marítimo del Istmo Centroamericano (USUARIOS).

12. The possible integration of financial services is the basis for Panama's renewed interest in the CACM.

13. For further comments on the potential of the relaunched CACM, see *El desafío del desarrollo centroamericano,* ed. Ennio Rodríguez (San José: EUNED, FEDEPRICAP, 1991).

14. FEDEPRICAP has compiled fragmentary evidence of investment in the CBI region being postponed until the outcome of the Mexican-NAFTA negotiations or canceled altogether. See FEDEPRICAP, "Informe de la visita de la delegación de FEDEPRICAP a Washington, D.C. el miércoles 20 y jueves 21 de noviembre de 1991, y reunión con la Embajadora Comercial de los Estados Unidos Carla Hills" (San José, 1991), mimeo, 7.

15. Ibid.

16. Ibid.

17. Fast track refers to special regulations for fast approval by Congress that prohibit direct changes to the proposed legislation.

18. FEDEPRICAP, 1991.

19. Static effects are the result of comparing, in terms of allocative efficiency, two states of equilibrium, before and after an FTA.

20. This argument is based on R. Bouzas, "La Iniciativa para las Américas y los países de América Latina y el Caribe: elementos para la formulación de políticas," mimeo, 1990 and J. M. Salazar and E. Lizano, "A Latina American Perspective on Free Trade in the Americas," paper prepared for the project "U.S.-Latin American Trade Relations in the 1990s," Overseas Development Council, mimeo, 1991.

21. A. M. El-Agraa, *The Theory and Measurement of International Economic Integration* (New York: St. Martin's Press, 1989).

22. "Dynamic effects" refers to the numerous factors influencing the rate of growth of the trading partners as a result of an FTA.

23. See El-Agraa, *Theory and Measurement of International Economic Integration,* 26–27.

24. R. J. Wonnacot, *The Economics of Overlapping Free Trade Areas and the Mexican Challenge* (Washington, D.C.: Canadian-American Committee, 1991).

25. Although relaunching the CACM includes a predetermined common external tariff for the beginning of 1993, there are also regional treaties covering intellectual property rights. A regional negotiation may become unavoidable at a certain point in time.

26. Honduras is about to complete the process of joining GATT.

27. For further commentary, see CEPAL, "La integración centroamericana frente a múltiples compromisos de negociación comercial," LC/MEX/R.377 (1992).

28. El Salvador has already ratified the protocol, and Honduras must now prepare a more complex law project adhering to the regional treaty on tariffs and customs.

29. FEDEPRICAP, 1991, 7.

30. Ibid.

31. The Guaranteed Access Levels provide virtually unlimited access for apparel and home furnishings produced in the CBI countries from fabrics formed and cut in the United States, provided the exporting country agrees to limit exports of nonqualifying apparel and home furnishings.

32. At the end of a five-year period, duties will be phased out on 96 percent of all yarns and threads, 95 percent of all fabrics, 83 percent of made-up articles, and 99 percent of all apparel.

33. CEPAL, 1992.

34. Additionally, there are specific rules for textiles, autos, televisions, computers, and some other products.

35. CEPAL, 1992.

36. "Report of GATT Working Party on U.S.-Canada FTA," *Inside U.S. Trade*, Special Report (November 29, 1991).

CARICOM:
Externally Vulnerable Regional Economic Integration

Richard L. Bernal

The Caribbean Common Market (Caricom) is an example of externally vulnerable integration. The economic development of the member states of Caricom, including the process of integration, has been dependent on and influenced to a considerable extent by external factors. For example, the level of interregional trade reflects much more the impact of external factors than the integration movement itself. This externally vulnerable economic integration process now confronts the dilemma of whether Caricom can further economic development. If the answer is in the affirmative, then it raises the question of whether to deepen or to widen the process. Further deepening among microeconomies will not produce the results intended and developments in the global economy and in the hemisphere suggest that widening is necessary.

Section I begins with an overview of the origins and objectives of Caricom. Then the structure and economic performance of Caricom member states are reviewed, complemented by an outline of the main features of intra-Caricom trade. The section culminates with a description of the current state of integration. Section II examines the current external context in which Caricom must operate and to which it must adapt, highlighting the implications of the North American Free Trade Agreement (NAFTA). Against this background, Section III analyzes the future of Caricom, focusing on the issues that derive from the dilemma of widening versus deepening. The policy imperatives are discussed in Section IV.

I. Caricom: A Review

Origins

Interest in the feasibility of political federation and economic union emerged in the Caribbean after World War I, but did not develop into a widely discussed idea until the late 1940s. This reflected a growing awareness of the West Indies as a group of societies that shared a common historical experience and distinct culture. The notion of economic and political union received further stimulus from the colonial civil service in Great Britain, which found the administration of these colonies easier to handle if treated as a group and with a common policy. During the 1950s a marked rise in nationalism in the West Indies led to persistent demands for independence from Britain. Also, in the late 1950s, a short-lived political federation of the West Indies left a legacy of economic collaboration and collective bargaining.[1] This, together with the acute awareness of the economic constraints of small size, led to the belief that regional integration could advance economic development.

The federation collapsed before any actual economic integration was implemented, but during 1965 the preliminary steps were taken toward the creation of a Caribbean Free Trade Association (CARIFTA) area. In 1967, CARIFTA was created, and the first integration measures took the form of lowering tariffs and quantitative restrictions in 1968. During the 1970s, intraregional trade expanded steadily and stimulated interest in moving from a free-trade area to a customs union. The Caribbean Community was established when Barbados, Guyana, Jamaica, and Trinidad and Tobago signed the Treaty of Chaguaramas on July 4, 1973. It currently comprises thirteen member countries, as Antigua and Barbuda, the Bahamas, Belize, Dominica, Grenada, Montserrat, St. Kitts and Nevis, Saint Lucia, and St. Vincent and the Grenadines, subsequently joined the original member states.

The initiative to form a free-trade area and then a common market came from academics and nationalist politicians, not from the business sector. However, subsequently, various business associations became active advocates and marshaled support in the region for a phased liberalization of trade. This vision of regional integration was accepted by the governments in the region in preference to an approach emphasizing the integration of production[2] by planned regional industrial programming.[3]

Objectives

The broad objectives of Caricom are:

1. To promote economic development, which was viewed as possible only if the degree of external dependence was reduced and some measure of economic sovereignty was reclaimed. The process of economic development necessarily involved structural transformation by industrialization, which would be made more viable by the increased size of the regional market and the efficiency generated by attaining economies of scale.

2. To increase bargaining power in negotiations in multilateral forums and bilateral negotiations, particularly with industrialized countries.

3. To achieve these goals while ensuring an equitable distribution of gains, or at least avoiding economic polarization between the more developed and the less developed states.

Structure of Caricom Economies

The Caribbean countries consist of very small economies, many of which are microstates, the smallest being Montserrat, with a population of 12,000 in an area of 103 sq. km. In fact, the total combined population of the thirteen countries is just under 6 million, spread over 270,000 sq. km. The gross domestic product (GDP) of the region is just over US$12 billion. For a statistical profile of Caricom member countries see Table 7.1. These economies are so minute that they have to be differentiated from the conventional concept of small economy, such as Singapore, with a GDP of $28 billion, or Hong Kong, with a population of 5.4 million. In these circumstances, small size is an additional constraint to development, which is reflected in the size of the market, narrow range of resources, and lack of economies of scale.

The member states of Caricom are individually and collectively vulnerable to external events. External vulnerability derives from economies with the following structural characteristics: (1) the small size; (2) the high degree of openness; e.g., trade/GDP ratio of over 70 percent and the import/GDP ratio ranging between 40–75 percent for most countries (see Table 7.1);

Table 7.1
Statistical Profile of Caricom, 1990

Country	Area (Km. Sq.)	1990 Population (thousands)	1990 GDP (US$M)	GDP per Capita (US$M)	Exports	Imports	External Debts	Imports/GDP
Antigua & Barbuda	442	84.0	418.7	4,985	16.7	230.7	260.1	55.1
Barbados	431	257.4	1,710.5	6,645	209.4	700.0	455.4	40.9
Belize	22,960	284.9	364.7	1,973	129.0	211.3	134.4	57.9
Dominica	750	83.5	171.2	2,050	54.9	117.9	78.2	68.9
Grenada	345	100.2	200.4	2,000	26.6	109.5	81.9	54.6
Guyana	214,970	7,544.0	256.3	340	268.1	310.9	1,713.0	121.3
Jamaica	11,424	2,403.5	3,993.8	1,662	1,156.9	1,877.1	4,280.0	47.0
Montserrat	103	12.0	73.6	6,133	1.7	34.7	2.7	47.1
St. Kitts & Nevis	269	42.9	152.7	3,560	19.0	102.0	36.4	66.8
St. Lucia	616	151.3	365.3	2,415	127.3	271.3	58.5	74.3
St. Vincent & The Grenadines	388	118.0	191.2	1,620	82.7	136.1	52.3	71.2
Trinidad & Tobago	5,128	1,227.4	4,970.6	4,050	2,080.5	1,261.6	2,012.0	25.4
TOTAL	257,826	5,419.5	12,869.0		4,172.8	5,363.1	9,164.9	

Source: *Statistical Profile of The Caribbean Community (Caricom)* (Black Rock, Barbados: The West Indian Commission, 1992).

(3) concentration on a few exports—in most instances, primary products such as bananas, sugar, and citrus or raw materials such as bauxite and oil; (4) dependency on a few extraregional markets, particularly industrialized countries such as the United States, which absorbed 43 percent of the region's exports and supplied 42 percent of its imports in 1990.[4] The Caribbean's trade and capital flows, both foreign investment and loans (concessional and commercial), are concentrated on the United States. Over 50 percent of the region's trade is with the United States, much of it under the Caribbean Basin Initiative (CBI). Most of the exports are marketed to the United States, Canada, and the European Economic Community (EEC) under preferential arrangements in the CBI, Canadian-Caribbean Agreements (Caribcan), and the Lôme Convention.

Economic Performance of Member States

The economies of Caricom member states experienced high and sustained growth in the 1960s, largely as a result of favorable market conditions for the principal exports, at a time when the world economy and industrialized countries were experiencing sustained economic growth. During the 1970s, a combination of adverse external developments affecting both export and import prices and internal economic management problems, caused a marked slowdown in economic growth, particularly in Jamaica, after the mid-1970s. The 1980s saw many economies in the region growing at very low rates, or experiencing contraction. Growth rates during 1983 to 1988 reveal slow growth or contraction in three of the larger, more developed economies. The United Nations Economic Commission for Latin America and the Caribbean (ECLAC) estimates that the average growth rate of real GDP was 0.9 percent for Jamaica, -1.4 percent for Guyana, and -3.0 percent for Trinidad and Tobago.[5] In fact, GDP per capita, at the end of the decade, was lower in some countries than it was in the late 1970s. Severe balance-of-payment crises and subsequent stabilization measures substantially reduced import capacity, which in turn led to a reduction in growth and export production. Bouts of high inflation, shortages of foreign exchange, and sizable exchange-rate depreciation compounded and aggravated the prevailing economic difficulties. Intraregional trade declined sharply and only began to recover in the late 1980s. However, economic recovery has been uneven and relatively weak.

Since the late 1970s countries like Jamaica, Guyana, and Trinidad and Tobago, and more recently Barbados, have had International Monetary Fund (IMF) stabilization programs and World Bank adjustment programs aimed at increasing growth, reducing the balance-of-payments deficit, and controlling inflation. Some Caricom countries have become heavily indebted during the last decade.[6] For many countries their debt is large in relation to their output and productive capacity. In Guyana, for example, the debt/GNP ratio is 522 percent. Servicing the external debt has become the single most sustained impediment to economic growth. The debt service ratio—i.e., the share of foreign exchange earnings from exports of goods and services required for debt payment—is high (e.g., in Jamaica, in 1988 it was 39.3 percent). The debt of the Caribbean region, as a whole, has more than doubled, from approximately US$6.1 billion in 1980 to US$14.3 billion in 1988. During the 1980s debt has more than doubled in Jamaica, Guyana, and Trinidad and Tobago. In Barbados, the debt has increased by 450 percent and in Antigua by 515 percent. The worsening situation is also evident in the increase in debt repayment by 50 percent during the years 1980 to 1988 from US$1.07 billion to US$1.56 billion. The most dramatic increases have been in Barbados, Jamaica, and the Bahamas, with increases of 352 percent, 215 percent, and 217 percent, respectively. As a result, negative net transfer of resources to foreign creditors has increased in the last few years.

Intra-Caricom Trade

Trade within regional integration arrangements experienced growth during the 1960s as it added renewed momentum to import substitution industrialization. The value of intraregional trade increased between the inception of CARIFTA in 1967 and 1974, shortly after the establishment of Caricom. During this period, Caricom became an increasingly important export market for the emergent manufacturing sectors of Barbados, Jamaica, and Trinidad and Tobago. Exports to Caricom, as a share of total exports, increased from 51.6 percent to 61.9 percent in Trinidad and Tobago during these years (see Table 7.2). The expansion of

Table 7.2

Exports to Caricom as a Percentage of Total Exports,
1967–1990

Country	1967	1974	1980	1990
Barbados	6.5	6.7	23.6	31.3
Guyana	23.0	13.5	13.2	6.1
Jamaica	12.3	14.2	5.9	6.2
Trinidad and Tobago	51.6	61.9	11.3	13.0
Antigua			31.5[a]	66.4
Belize			6.1	8.0
Dominica			61.5	25.2
Grenada			11.1	22.6
Montserrat			60.6	33.8
St. Kitts			18.2	18.3
St. Lucia			38.2	18.1
St. Vincent			43.3	31.6

[a] 1984

Source: *The Commonwealth Caribbean: The Integration Experience* (Baltimore: Johns Hopkins University Press, for the World Bank, 1978), 30, and *Statistical Profile of the Caribbean Community (Caricom)* (Black Rock, Barbados: The West Indian Commission, 1992), 4–5.

intraregional trade stalled during the 1970s and contracted sharply during the 1980s. Between 1980 and 1990, Caricom declined in importance as both an export and import market. Exports to Caricom as a share of total exports declined for six countries, was virtually unchanged for three others, and increased in only three countries (see Table 7.2).

Caricom as a source of imports has declined significantly, as its share in total exports has decreased for eleven of the twelve member states (see Table 7.3). Intraregional exports as a share of total merchandise exports (excluding petroleum) have fluctuated between 5 and 8 percent since the integration of Caricom.[7] During the 1980s, petroleum accounted for 20 to 60 percent of intraregional exports,[8] which means that non-petroleum exports within Caricom are extremely small. Since agricultural products

Table 7.3

Imports from Caricom as a Percentage of Total Imports,
1967–1990

Country	1967	1974	1980	1990
Barbados	14.0	15.6	19.0	15.5
Guyana	26.9	29.7	39.5	20.0
Jamaica	9.3	31.4	7.3	4.7
Trinidad and Tobago	26.7	13.2	6.4	6.2
Antigua			22.6[a]	10.9
Belize			1.6	6.2
Dominica			26.8	21.3
Grenada			32.8	23.5
Montserrat			21.8[b]	15.6
St. Kitts			20.1	15.1
St. Lucia			20.9	17.9
St. Vincent			20.0	20.8

[a] 1984

[b] 1981

Source: *The Commonwealth Caribbean: The Integration Experience* (Baltimore: Johns Hopkins University Press, for the World Bank, 1978), 30, and *Statistical Profile of the Caribbean Community (Caricom)* (Black Rock, Barbados: The West Indian Commission, 1992), 4–5.

and foodstuffs account for 25 to 30 percent of intra-Caricom exports, manufacturing exports are minute. Intra-Caricom exports increased, on average, by 20 percent per annum during the years 1973–80. The value of intraregional exports declined by 53 percent between 1980 and 1986, and in 1990 it was still 31 percent below the 1980 level. During the 1980s, regional integration schemes and regional trade agreements either ceased to exist or limped along in name, rather than in reality.

The contraction of trade and the disintegration of regional arrangements were due to the following factors: (1) collapse of regional payment arrangements; (2) lack of macroeconomic policy coordination; (3) reluctance to relinquish some economic sover-

eignty; (4) policy disparities due to widely different political phi-
losophies and economic development strategies; (5) adverse impact of external shocks such as oil prices and declining commodity
prices; (6) protectionist policies and the use of exchange controls;
(7) exchange rate volatility; and (8) the contraction of import
demand as a result of adjustment and debt.

Current State of Integration

At their tenth meeting, held in Grenada in July 1989, the
heads of government of the Caribbean Community adopted the
Grand Anse Declaration and Work Programme for the Advancement of the Integration Movement. More specifically, they agreed
to establish a common market as early as possible. They decided
to:

(1) establish a schedule for implementation of the three
Common Market Instruments required by the Treaty of
Chaguaramas: the Common External Tariff; the Rules
of Origin; and a Harmonized Scheme of Fiscal Incentives;

(2) sign the agreement establishing the Caricom Industrial
Programming Scheme (CIPS);

(3) enact the necessary legislation to implement the CIPS
and the Caricom Enterprise Regime (CER);

(4) liberalize the movement of capital, starting with cross-
listing and trading of securities on existing stock ex-
changes;

(5) commence technical studies on the establishment of a
regional equity-venture capital fund;

(6) intensify consultation and cooperation on monetary,
financial, and exchange rate policies;

(7) increase policy coordination at the macroeconomic, sectoral, and project levels;

(8) implement arrangements for the free movement of
skilled and professional personnel;

(9) re-examine the ideas of a system of air and sea carriers;
and

(10) strengthen collective effort at joint overseas representation and in international negotiations.

Most of these measures have not yet been fully implemented, despite the time limits originally proposed. The Caricom Industrial Programming Scheme was implemented in September 1989, and it was agreed to enact legislation to implement the Caricom Enterprise Regime. In 1989 the heads of government also approved the Caribbean Community Programme for Agricultural Development. The objective of this program is to achieve a higher level of food security. The agreement on a harmonized scheme of fiscal incentives was revised in order to incorporate provisions to support the development of the agricultural and service sectors, including tourism. The new scheme contains proposals that guarantee exceptions, a reduction of import duties, tax exemption, and credit. The West Indian Commission, in its 1992 report "Time for Action," made six recommendations for immediate action:

(1) To ease the difficulties of traveling in the region, Caricom citizens should be allowed to present other regulated forms of identification (incorporating a photograph) other than passports.

(2) Skilled and professional West Indians should be allowed to move freely in the region, starting with accredited media workers, and all graduates of the University of West Indies and of other recognized institutions.

(3) Take steps to create a common currency, since it would serve to eliminate transaction costs of national currency conversions and exchange-rate uncertainties in trade and investment decisions, thus facilitating the free movement of goods and services. Investigate the feasibility of an independent regional Caribbean Monetary Authority which could issue a Caribbean currency.

(4) Establish a Caribbean Investment Fund, by setting up a team of financial experts to begin negotiations with prospective business sponsors.

(5) Complete the implementation of the Common External Tariff (CET), the Rules of Origin, and the Harmonized Scheme of Fiscal Incentives, as the three principal instruments for creating a common market.

(6) Mobilize for International Negotiations: Expertise available at the Caricom Secretariat should be supplemented

by a facility enabling the authorities responsible for the negotiations to draw, if need be, on the technical skills scattered throughout the region.

Caricom is not a common market or a customs union, as the CET has not yet been implemented. The main objective of the CET is to provide regional protection to agriculture and industry in order to develop a productive structure that may compete in third markets. The CET, and the rules of origin, are aimed at expanding industrialization by means of increased utilization of input available in the region. The original intention of the external policy, using the Common Protective Policy, was to provide a level of protection within the common market for companies producing in that market. However, this policy orientation was changed in 1984, when the Caricom heads of government agreed that: (a) policy will aim at a greater outward orientation of the manufacturing sector; (b) the CET should replace, over a phased period, quantitative restrictions as the principal instrument of protection in the Caribbean Common Market; and (c) that the Secretariat should undertake the necessary technical work to substitute CET rates for national quantitative restrictions against third countries. The revised CET, with a classification structure based on the Harmonized Commodity Description and Coding system (HS), and the changes in the rules of origin, became effective January 1, 1991. To date, nine of the twelve member countries have implemented the CET.

Participants at the Fourth Inter-Sessional Meeting of the Conference of Heads of Government of the Caribbean Community, held March 22–23, 1993, made three major decisions: (a) the revised CET and the Rules of Origin would be introduced by June 30, 1993, and all remaining barriers to intraregional trade should also be removed by that date, which is preparatory to the creation of a single market; (b) the establishment of the Council of Governors of the Central Banks of the Caribbean Community, which represents a staged approach to the creation of a monetary union; and (c) the negotiations toward establishing a Caribbean Investment Fund reached an advanced stage and it was agreed that member states would take all the necessary measures to facilitate the completion of the process of establishing the fund at the earliest possible date.

Caricom: An Evaluation

First, the objective of economic development and structural transformation is yet to be attained. Economic vulnerability arising from small size and the structural characteristics of Caricom economies has remained virtually unchanged despite the existence of Caricom since 1973. Second, the objective of collaboration in collective bargaining has become an established practice, which has undoubtedly improved the bargaining power of these countries. Third, the objective of equitable distribution of benefits is very difficult to evaluate. Judged by distribution of industry, there does seem to be polarization. However, growth rates of GDP and per-capita income show the smaller, so-called less-developed countries exceeding that of some larger, more developed countries, but they pose the question of whether deepening should precede, follow, or accompany widening.

Structurally rooted economic vulnerability has resisted modification through regional integration, primarily because Caricom is still not a common market. This process has severe limitations, because aggregation of small economies still yields a critical mass that in many respects is inadequate. Even if more progress had been made on deepening integration, the total regional market may still not have attained the critical mass to ensure development and transformation. This clearly suggests the need to enlarge Caricom by widening its membership.

II. The Current External Context

Globalization

In recent years, international trade and capital flows have grown at a faster rate than world gross domestic product (GDP). This reflects the progressive globalization of production and finance, which is pressuring governments to minimize, harmonize, or eliminate national barriers (such as tariffs, quotas, exchange controls) to the international movement of goods, services, capital, and finance. The driving force impelling globalization is transnational corporate integration through mergers, strategic corporate alliances, and takeovers. Efficiency in resource allocation and profit maximization on a global scale cannot be attained within a world economy fractured into national economies. Transnational corporate integration impels multicountry market integration, initially in a regional context, both as ex-post economic rationalization and as a defense by the nation-state against the inevitable relinquishing of the vestiges of economic sovereignty.

Trade Blocs

The transition to a world market is taking place by way of national economies merging and amalgamating into trade blocs. Trade blocs are created both by deliberate policies of integration among groups of like-minded governments and by the unplanned concentration of trade and investment among countries, often creating a commonality of interest. The formalization of the EEC as a common market added impetus to the nascent trend toward economic blocs by setting in motion a defensive, reactive response to counter this development by forming rival blocs.

Stalled Multilateral Trade Liberalization

The difficulties experienced in completing the prolonged negotiations of the Uruguay Round of the General Agreement on Trade and Tariffs (GATT) continue unabated. The Round could end in disarray, or fail to resolve key issues of the agenda. A collapse or partial resolution could spark an escalation of protectionism, characterized by an acceleration of countries forming trade blocs. It also is possible that the disintegration of GATT negotiations could provoke a proliferation of bilateral trade arrangements and intensify the tendency to form various regional trade arrangements, which by virtue of a common external tariff may raise protectionist barriers to exports from other groups and countries.

Revival of Regionalism in the Western Hemisphere

There has been a resurgence of interest in regional trade liberalization, regional integration, and cooperation in the Caribbean and Latin America.[9] This momentum actually preceded the U.S. Enterprise for the Americas Initiative; the enterprise did not initiate these developments, but rather complemented them, and may have added a catalyst to accelerate the process. This resurgence of interest in regional trade arrangements and regional integration has been influenced by global and regional developments. The need for a response to the formation of trade blocs in a "regionalized" world economy provided strong impetus to the new wave of integration. Regional integration is viewed as a potent response because it strengthens bargaining power and coordinates external policies.

Erosion of Preferential Trade Arrangements

A world economy compartmentalized into trade blocs creates an atmosphere for international economic relations in which negotiated reciprocity and tradeoffs among developed economies is the order of the day. This is rationalized by a philosophy that, in the pursuit of free trade, all countries are better off through trade negotiations at the multilateral, plurilateral, or bilateral level. Corporate integration also adds pressure to standardize regulatory regimes throughout the world. There is less sympathy and tolerance in developed countries for preferential trade arrangements for developing countries or for exemptions or differentials in GATT. The result is either a shift toward reciprocity (as is evident in the difference between the CBI and the approach to the Enterprise for the Americas Initiative and NAFTA) or expansion of preferences from a select group to a larger number of countries or all countries.

Associated with these developments is a trend toward expanding the number of countries eligible for preferential trade arrangements both in the Lômé Convention and the CBI. Already the benefits of CBI have been extended to the Andean Pact countries, and the NAFTA will provide improved market-access conditions to Mexico, which supersede those provided by the CBI. It is a distinct possibility that Central and Latin American countries could be given the same access to the banana market of the EEC, Caricom, and African, Caribbean, and Pacific countries. Given that their cost of production is much lower than that of other Caribbean producers, the effect could be serious for Caricom countries.

Implications of NAFTA

The Enterprise for the Americas Initiative, which consists of three components—debt relief, trade liberalization, and investment promotion—has been hailed as both timely and innovative, because it proposes to address the major economic problems of Latin America and the Caribbean. It was launched at the culmination of a decade of economic decline in that region. The NAFTA, recently concluded between the United States, Canada, and Mexico, will constitute the first building block of the trade component of the Enterprise of the Americas Initiative.

The implementation of NAFTA would put CBI countries at a disadvantage in terms of access to U.S. markets, likely resulting in the following:

(1) The elimination of quota and phase-out of tariffs on Mexican products could cause a diversion of U.S. demand from suppliers in CBI countries to firms in Mexico, thus reducing CBI exports. This would inadvertently create a situation in which Mexico—which already has inexpensive labor and energy, lower transportation costs, and economies of scale—would now have a further advantage over the CBI countries.

(2) Diversion of investment is already evident; in the last two years there has been a pause in regional investment, as investors waited to evaluate the NAFTA provisions. A report of the U.S. International Trade Commission (USITC) concluded that "NAFTA will introduce incentives that will tend to favor apparel investment shifts away from the Caribbean Basin Economic Recovery Act countries to Mexico."[10]

(3) There is danger that existing productive capacity will relocate or close, particularly in "footloose" industries that can easily be relocated.

(4) It would be ironic if 110,000 trade-related jobs in the United States, which are maintained by exports to the CBI region, were to be lost as a result of investment diversion and trade contraction resulting from the erosion of the CBI caused by NAFTA. Trade and investment diversion could stymie the growth momentum in the Caribbean, marginalizing the region from the economic dynamic in its main export market—the United States. However, this development would be prevented if appropriate policy measures were adopted by the United States.

Caricom's Response to NAFTA

The governments of Caricom countries need to lobby for nondiscriminatory access to the U.S. market to ensure a level

playing field. The NAFTA could convert the CBI into a depreci-
ated asset by superseding CBI provisions, and thereby placing
these small, undiversified economies at a competitive disadvantage
in terms of their access to the U.S. market. Remedial action is
urgently required to prevent an adverse impact of CBI countries
and preserve the relative value of CBI status. The following policy
measures should constitute an appropriate U.S. policy.[11]

1. *Parity as a transitional arrangement.* The CBI countries
should have the same conditions of market access to the United
States provided to Mexico under the NAFTA. Specifically, CBI
countries and Mexico should receive simultaneous and equivalent
treatment in terms of tariffs, rules of origin, and quota elimination.
This would involve upgrading CBI to cover those products that
are exempt from duty-free treatment under CBI, and those goods
and services placed at a disadvantage vis-à-vis Mexico by the
provisions of NAFTA. For example, under current conditions, the
textile and apparel sector of CBI countries will have to compete
for market share and for investment with a Mexican textile
and apparel sector that will face reduced restrictions in the U.S.
market, and no restrictions at all after ten years.

Parity as a transitional arrangement will enable the economies of the CBI region to complete their process of economic
reform and structural adjustment, putting them in a position to
move toward full reciprocity. A premature attempt by the CBI
countries to provide full reciprocity could be detrimental to the
process of adjustment, since export-led growth is only possible
with stable market access. The period of time necessary to attain
a position where reciprocity can be provided will vary among
economies depending on their size, level of development, and
economic structure.

2. *Phased reciprocity over a suitable adjustment period.* Having used a transitional period based on similar market access to
that provided to Mexico under NAFTA, CBI countries will be in
a position to begin to phase in reciprocity over a suitable period.
A suitable adjustment period will take account of the small size
and undiversified structure of Caribbean economies. Furthermore,
reciprocity should not be given a restrictive connotation. That is,
reciprocity does not mean strict equivalence in tariff reduction or
elimination of quantitative restrictions, but must reflect the range
of issues encompassed in international economic relations;

namely, trade in goods and services, investment, and intellectual property rights. The form, specifics, and pace of reciprocity should be worked out between the United States and the CBI countries through the institutional mechanism of the Trade and Investment Framework Agreements and the Caricom-U.S. Joint Council on Trade and Investment.

III. The Future of Caricom: Deepening Versus Widening

If Caricom is to achieve all its aims — in particular economic development and concomitant structural transformation — it must resolve the issue of deepening versus widening. Regional integration was superimposed on the economic structure of Caribbean economies in a purposeful attempt to restructure these economies, reduce external dependency, internalize the dynamic of economic growth, and change the role of the Caricom countries in the international division of labor. However, apart from the manufacturing sector, Caricom has a tenuous or peripheral connection to the function and performance of Caribbean economies. It is usually asserted that in order for Caricom to have more impact on trade and economic growth, it is necessary to deepen the integration process. However, deepening seems to hold little prospect of reducing vulnerability to external events, given the small size of the market, even after full integration, and also because of the absence of corporate development in production integration. In addition, the factors that have inhibited deepening in the past persist in the present, and optimism is unwarranted. Some of the benefits to be attained by deepening may be more forthcoming through judicious widening. Therefore, widening should become a priority and should no longer await the completion or advancement of deepening, because deepening will not reduce vulnerability to external events.

There has been a strong resistance to widening Caricom, despite repeated expressions of interest and formal requests by non-English–speaking Caribbean countries. Surinam was granted observer status in CARIFTA in March 1973 and subsequently participated in some ministerial meetings. In 1982 it applied for observer status in the heads of government meetings, the Common Market Council, and the organs of the Caribbean Community. In

1974, Caricom signed an agreement establishing a Caricom-Mexico joint commission, but little has transpired. Also in 1974, Haiti applied for membership in the community and associate membership in the Common Market, but this was not granted. The application was amended to that of permanent observer in the community and in the Caribbean Development Bank in October 1982. The Dominican Republic asked for admission to observer status in institutions of functional cooperation in May 1982. In 1993, a Venezuela-Caricom agreement went into effect, providing one-way free entry to the Venezuelan market with Caricom reciprocating after five years.

There are two reasons for the reluctance to widen: first, an unwillingness to introduce a greater degree of heterogeneity into a group which already has such a wide diversity of perceptions; and second, the towering fear of being overpowered by larger, more developed countries, which no doubt strikes the raw nerve of the colonial experience deep in the collective psyche. This poses a dilemma which has produced political caution and administrative inertia. Small size, individually and collectively, requires widening to enlarge the market and increase bargaining leverage in negotiations, but this would involve larger countries and would reduce the influence of Caricom countries in collective decision making. The dilemma can only be resolved when the intellectual gridlock is broken. Ideally this will occur from within the region, rather than from external shocks or policy initiatives.

In its aptly titled report, *Time for Action*, The West Indian Commission (WIC) stated:

> the widening of Caricom's relations into the entire Caribbean must be an essential part of the way forward. But we believe it would be a mistake to see that process of widening simply in terms of enlarging Caricom's membership. There are important factors to be balanced. On the economic side, we have to feel our way in enlarging the Caricom market so that we make progress in that direction without being lost within our own widened Community.

The WIC proposed "a new Association of Caribbean States, the A.C.S., anchored on Caricom and promoted by Caricom. As the largest integration movement in the Caribbean, we have a responsibility to take the initiative."[12]

Deepening

While the priority should be on widening, this must be accompanied by deepening, two important aspects of which are:

(1) Intraregional corporate integration. Caricom must prepare a strategy for its survival and development in the new world economic and political context. This depends not only on the policies of governments, but on the readiness and ability of the private sector to compete effectively. The expansion of exports will depend on a combination of comparative and competitive advantages. The state of preparedness between sectors varies considerably, reflecting economic and psychological factors. The fact that activities such as bauxite exports and tourism are competitive in price and quality proves the capability to compete in the global marketplace.

Whether the Caribbean economies are able to take advantage of an enlarged regional market to expand exports depends not only on the policies of governments, but on the readiness and ability of the private sector to compete effectively. Even where Caribbean economies have a comparative advantage it could, as in the past, be offset by the lack of a competitive advantage by locally owned firms. In the larger, more advanced economies such as Jamaica and Trinidad and Tobago, some firms and financial institutions have become Caribbean multinationals or are branching into the United States, Great Britain, and Cuba, and there are some entrepreneurs whose horizons are hemispheric and even global. In fact, it is the outgrowth of the national market and the process of corporate integration which, like in the EEC, is driving the resurgence of regional trade liberalization, including that of Caricom.

In the microeconomies, the private sector firms are economic minutiae, family owned and managed, and almost wholly and profitably confined to commerce rather than production—except in the traditional agricultural exports, such as bananas. Even a trans-island merger movement would not make them viable, but there is no reason why they cannot be worthwhile joint-venture partners with foreign investors. Apart from infrastructure, all other inputs including technology can be purchased. The difficulties are not insurmountable, but there must be both a recognition and a willingness. This, like every process of adjustment, begins with a change of mind, outlook, and attitude.

(2) Financial integration. Progress toward economic integration in the real aspects of Caribbean economies has not been accompanied by the appropriate level of integration in the financial sphere. Finance, as used here, refers to the institutions, financial markets, and financial policies that facilitate and influence the process of financial intermediation. There should be complementarity between the levels of development in real and financial aspects of regional economic integration, because financial development can facilitate and promote real economic development.

Two levels of financial integration exist: capital market and monetary. Capital market integration is the process by which capital markets, which are geographically and nationally distinct, combine to function as a single, multinational capital market. Monetary integration involves integrating financial systems and establishing institutions to regulate the resulting integrated financial system. Monetary integration involves a single currency (or exchange-rate union), a common central bank, harmonized monetary policy, a common reserve pool, and the absence of exchange controls. Capital market integration is less difficult to operationalize and therefore precedes monetary integration. The quintessence of a common market is free movement of the factors of production, to which the free movement of money and capital is the logical complement. Capital market integration is the level of financial development appropriate to a common market such as Caricom. Apart from promoting financial development and economic growth possibilities, it could assist in reducing the polarization that characterizes Caricom at present. The objective of capital market integration within Caricom is to create a single regional capital market, which can promote the region's economic development. Such integration promises significant potential advantages, with some offsetting drawbacks, most of which can be minimized, if not eliminated.

There are five main advantages to be gained from an integrated Caribbean capital market:

(a) It would permit countries to supplement their domestic savings from savings within the region in times of deficit and to export savings in times of excess. Hence, the savings for the Caribbean countries would be allocated within the framework of regional optimum, rather than national optimum.

(b) Integration should mean increased mobility of funds between individual, national capital markets and could thereby reduce the outflow of capital funds from the region, including capital
flight. Some overseas placement of Caribbean funds may have
occurred because of the lack of intraregional mobility of funds,
rather than because of better investment opportunities outside the
region. This is particularly the case with financial institutions in
the less developed countries where at present these institutions are
unable to obtain local securities of a sufficiently wide variety to
enable them to operate a balanced portfolio.

(c) It would permit financial institutions to undertake a larger
volume of business and so achieve economies of scale.

(d) It would allow financial institutions to diversify their asset
portfolios by increasing and broadening their options by allowing
them to choose from securities available in the region rather than
just national securities.

(e) Capital market integration will improve the process of
financial intermediation, offering a wider variety of instruments
and institutions. Better financial intermediation would generate a
larger volume of savings, since a multiplicity of savings media in
the form of different types of financial instruments and service help
to increase savings.

Widening

Expanding Caricom or joining a major trade bloc. Developing economies, and in particular small countries, need a liberal
multilateral trading system because they are highly dependent on
trade. Given the type of products exported by small developing
economies, access to the markets of industrialized countries is
necessary for their economic survival. The emergence of trade
blocs reduces the shift away from preferential access and the lack
of progress in the Uruguay Round of the GATT, representing the
collapse of a rule-based multilateral trade regime. This forces small
developing countries to evaluate very carefully the costs of exclusion from participation in one or more trade blocs. For the Caricom countries, the question is whether it can continue to have
membership in CBI, Caribcan, and Lômé. Would participation
in the Lômé Convention and NAFTA be compatible? What is
the relationship of NAFTA and the Enterprise for the Americas

Initiative, and their compatibility with existing trade arrangements such as the Lômé Convention and Caribcan, to which the Caribbean countries are members? For example, in accordance with Article 174 [2(a)] of the Lômé Convention, "ACP States . . . shall grant to the Community treatment no less favorable than most-favored-nation treatment."[13] This means that any trade concession extended to the United States by Caricom must also be extended to the EEC.

Countries not included or associated with major trading blocs could face steep protectionist barriers, and be marginalized from the growth-stimulating dynamic of the industrialized countries. There has to be a detailed process of evaluation of the costs and benefits of participating in or staying outside of a major trade bloc.

Should Caricom integrate with a larger trading bloc, or deepen Caricom, or try to have the best of all worlds by participating in the Lômé Convention, CBI, and Caribcan? Deepening Caricom does not seem to be a viable strategy, since further integration will be difficult and, even if achieved, may not provide a basis for sustained economic development. Whether overlapping, preferential trade arrangements can be retained and their compatibility maintained are issues over which Caricom exercises very little influence. The likely options appear to be those within the Western Hemisphere, which in reality are limited to accession to an expanded NAFTA or joining a rejuvenated Latin American Free Trade Association (LAFTA). The latter seems some way off, and history does not offer any encouragement for the belief that such an integration scheme will function in the foreseeable future. The option of accession or association with NAFTA could present itself in a year or two. Defensive motives may prevail, as being outside of NAFTA would make exporting to that market even more difficult. In addition, there is the pull factor of the concentration of trade between the United States and Caricom. In the long run, Caricom's major trade links will be with the Western Hemisphere.

The emergence of a Western Hemisphere trade bloc may be already occurring as interdependence within the Western Hemisphere has increased tremendously. For example, in the United States, about 35 percent of total exports go to countries within the hemisphere (28 percent goes to Canada and Mexico — the prospective members of NAFTA—and 7 percent to the rest of the hemisphere). For Caricom countries, about one-half of their exports go to the United States. The rate of growth of U.S. exports to the hemisphere has far exceeded the growth of exports to the rest of the world. Similarly, trade within the hemisphere has grown much more rapidly for Latin American countries than trade with the rest of the world.

If Caricom has the option of integrating with a larger trade bloc, should the Caricom countries proceed as individual countries, or should there be collective participation? If collective participation is available and feasible given the differences in readiness, what collection of countries should proceed? Should this be Caricom or some wider version of the Caribbean? Collective participation seems logical, given that it would increase the negotiating leverage of Caricom. However, it may prove difficult because differences in readiness could mean moving at the pace of the country that is least willing or able.

Accommodating developmental heterogeneity. How are the persistent differences in levels of economic development to be accommodated within Caricom and in any wider integration group, particularly where developed countries are involved? Within Caricom, the less developed countries are given concessions in the form of longer adjustment periods and less stringent rules of origin. Indeed, polarization has not been a divisive problem among Caricom countries, as per-capita income for many of the so-called less developed countries compares favorably with the supposedly more developed. However, the question of different levels of development is of paramount importance in Caricom's participation in CBI, Caribcan, and the Lômé Convention. It will also assume considerable importance if Caricom extends membership to countries like the Dominican Republic and Venezuela, or if Caricom countries opt to join regional groupings, which include larger or more developed economies. This was one of the most contentious issues in negotiating framework agreements, even though they are nonbinding, committing the signatories only to further dialogue. That difference of outlook was resolved in the case of the U.S.-Caricom Framework Agreement by the term "undiversified economies," which tried to grapple with the fact that because of the very narrow range of production and exports, Caribbean economies have a structural vulnerability to external events and are in urgent need of structural adjustment. The United States has continued to maintain that there can be no long-term accommodation of different levels of development in a "mature relationship." Some flexibility will be necessary, however, since any regional arrangement aimed at integration and/or trade liberalization must accommodate development heterogeneity, at least initially. This includes different levels of development, coexistence of a variety of growth strategies and structural adjustment at varying stages of completion. Indeed, this is recognized and reflected in the Caricom and the EEC, and was conceded by the United States when it granted developing-country status to Israel in the U.S.-Israel Free Trade Agreement.

Adjustment period. The period of adjustment is critical and can be general, sectional, or product specific. Product- or sector-specific adjustment periods, if sufficiently long, will allow these small, "undiversified" economies to implement orderly economic reorganization. Caribbean fears may be exaggerated since for some sectors, the U.S.-Canada Free Trade Agreement has a phase-in period as long as ten years. In addition, only a limited number of products would require prolonged adjustment periods or exemptions, because production is concentrated on a narrow range of goods and services and exports consist, in many cases, of a few primary products. Sensitive products can be handled by "snapback provisions," which permit, under specified conditions, the imposition of a temporary duty. There can also be safeguards such as Article 1101 of the U.S.-Canada Free Trade Agreement, which allows that during the transition period, either country may respond to serious injury to domestic producers resulting from the reduction of duties under the FTA by restoring tariffs for a period of no longer than three years.

The misconception is that disparities in size and levels of development can be addressed simply by extending the period of adjustment or by excluding certain products and sectors and thereby protecting them. Neither of these really helps the countries as a group, or individually, to get to the stage of being efficient or competitive.

Asymmetrical reciprocity. Reciprocity can have a range of connotations, which cannot be reduced to equivalence, but can be a modified or conditional "most-favored-nation" treatment. Asymmetrical adjustment is one way to recognize and compensate for differences in the levels of development. The notion of differential treatment is deeply entrenched in the smaller, less developed countries, which receive longer adjustment periods even within Caricom. It will be difficult to disabuse these countries of this tenet of their philosophy of development, but few will oppose the concept of phasing out differences in obligations over a long period, perhaps twenty years. Clearly, at the outset of an FTA it would be difficult to establish special and differential treatment in perpetuity. Therefore, specific criteria for graduation to nondiscriminatory status with mutuality of concessions will be needed. The United States has both espoused "graduation" and practiced it by disqualifying certain advanced developing countries from the Generalized System of Preferences.

Should reciprocity be complete or asymmetrical, partial or "relative," and should it commence immediately or be phased in over a period of years? The Caribbean's apprehension of immediate and complete reciprocity derives less from the inability to undertake policy measures and institutional changes, but more from the social and economic costs of structural adjustment. This is a valid concern because in these economies, structural adjustment implies both resource allocation from declining to emerging or growing sectors, and resource creation for the installment of new or upgraded productive capacity. There are risks and difficulties involved in improving quality, quantity, and price in order to survive and compete in the vast hemispheric market with a range of competitors, which include some of the giant multinational corporations, whose assets and sales dwarf the GDP of the combined Caribbean countries. Daunting as this appears, it can be accomplished, because reducing the production process into smaller, discrete processes provides opportunities, and there are specialized niches in the international division of labor that can be filled by relatively small-scale operations.

Increasing collective bargaining power. Regional integration was advocated as a means of enhancing economic sovereignty through collective action in bargaining with the industrialized countries, in multilateral forums such as GATT and with the multilateral corporations. Many in the region believe that, given major changes in world trade such as Europe 1992, NAFTA, and the Uruguay Round of the GATT, Caricom needs to participate in a larger bargaining unit. Girvan regards it as "unthinkable that any Caribbean state acting singly, or even jointly in Caricom, could hope to cope adequately with such negotiations."[14] The experience of regional cooperation has been encouraging, but this can be achieved without regional integration.

IV. Policy Imperatives

Enhanced Competitiveness through Adjustment

It is frequently claimed that regional trade liberalization schemes are a preparatory stage to competing in the world market. This, however, may be a misconception in cases where (1) regional integration involves small economies, all of which produce the same products, and integration does not improve efficiency because the regional market is not enlarged sufficiently to provide economies of scale; (2) most of the major exports of member countries are sold in extraregional markets (for example, integrating the markets of Caricom economies will have little impact on increasing exports of apparel, sugar, bauxite, oil, banana, coffee, and tourism); and (3) the process of regional integration by production integration is retarded by wide disparities among member countries in policy, size, and development.

The countries of the Caricom region must face the fact that preferential trade arrangements, such as the CBI, the Lôme Convention, and Caribcan, will not exist indefinitely. The region must adapt to eroding or disappearing preferential trade regimes. In order to survive in a rapidly changing, globalizing, world economy, Caricom countries must redouble their efforts at structural adjustment, seeking ways to improve and enhance productivity and efficiency. The Caricom countries have rich potential and are capable of successfully competing in quality and price in the global marketplace. Growth-oriented adjustment depends on access to export markets; the process of internal adjustment and export market access must proceed in tandem.

Many Caricom countries are implementing programs of market-oriented reforms, and the success of this adjustment process will largely depend on increased investment and export growth. Several Caricom countries are well advanced in a process of economic adjustment which will enable them to compete more effectively in the global market. Domestic economic reforms can be enhanced and brought to fruition by improved export market access for new and traditional exports. Legislative and other action should be taken to ensure that the CBI countries retain their relative advantage in the U.S. and Canadian markets in the medium term.

Export Reorientation

The process of adjustment will only commence in earnest when there is a change in attitude and outlook, when Caricom entrepreneurs dare to think the new and adventurous. For example, since the early 1950s succeeding governments have viewed the transition from underdevelopment to development as a process of industrialization, progressing from import-substitution industrialization to the export of manufactured goods. But despite protection and other government support, this transition has not taken place. Developments in the world economy and the success of the newly industrialized countries of Asia suggest this is no longer a viable strategy. Perhaps Caricom should skip the traditional development by industrialization, and pursue development by the export of services. This strategy has distinct advantages: the service sector is the fastest growing sector in world trade and in the U.S. economy, which is Caricom's largest trading partner. The jobs created would be relatively high wage and environmentally safe.

Innovative entrepreneurs must look beyond traditional economic activities and to financial services and to the new dynamic sectors in the global economy, such as microelectronics, biotechnology, telecommunications, robotics, and information. These sectors will require a work force that is more skilled, knowledge oriented, and capable of adopting new technology.[15] Management, production, and decision making will have to be "informationalized."[16]

There is no need to panic, because there are plenty of opportunities to earn foreign exchange and provide employment for Caribbean nationals. To illustrate, the high cost of health care in the United States makes it less expensive for someone to fly to the Caribbean for treatment. All operations other than open-heart surgery could be done in the Caribbean at a fraction of the U.S. cost. Patients could enjoy a holiday in the sun while they recuperate, and still save money. The day is coming when there will be multinational hospitals. A hospital in Washington, D.C., may own an affiliate in the Caribbean, to which it would refer all cases requiring certain types of surgery, such as cosmetic and reconstructive, and certain forms of rehabilitative treatment. Retirement homes for people requiring custodial care is another potential market. These enterprises would permit our doctors and nurses to earn foreign exchange, stemming the loss of medical personnel and rebuilding the health service.

Export Market Penetration

Responsiveness to market changes. Export firms in Caricom will have to develop the capacity to respond quickly to changes in demand in existing and new markets —in particular, that of the United States. More than anything else, this is the secret of success of the newly industrialized export economies of Asia. If product *x* is demanded today, Japan will manufacture it tomorrow and her neighbors will produce it at a lower price the following day. This ability to respond quickly to changes in the marketplace determines the success of exports. Improvements in the speed of telecommunications and information technology has resulted in instant information, which requires and makes possible immediate decision making.[17]

Strategic corporate alliances. Caricom exporters have suffered in the past from having to deal with middlemen to penetrate the distribution chain in foreign export markets. It is paramount that this obstacle be removed as quickly as possible. The obvious solution is for large exporters or groups of exporters to purchase or establish retail outlets in major export markets. Caribbean exporters are often extremely small, and therefore at a severe disadvantage, compared to the firms and multinational corporations against which they compete in world markets. Thus there is a need for mergers and strategic alliances[18] to provide a larger capital base and pool of resources and expertise. After studying trends in international industries, Doz concludes that collaborative agreements and strategic partnerships may deeply modify the nature of global competition and the organization of international production by "creating a series of intermediate positions between national and global competitors."[19]

Improving Productivity

Entrepreneurship in Caricom exhibits very uneven development, but in some countries such as Jamaica, a new brand of entrepreneurship has emerged in recent years. Increasingly, entrepreneurs are competing in the world market and building multinational corporations by establishing overseas factories, banks, building societies, and hotels. They are demonstrating new capability, innovation, technical sophistication, and informed risk taking. However, the most difficult and most important determinant of price and quality competitiveness, of speedy response to changes in demand, and of efficient marketing and distribution is the quality of human resources. There are three aspects of the human resource dimension: entrepreneurship, management, and the productivity of workers.

Management will have to become more sophisticated, be constantly in touch with developments in international markets, and constantly update itself on new technological innovations. Caribbean managerial capacity has improved considerably and professionalism has increased in recent years. However, there is still room for improvement, and the region needs to upgrade the management capacity of the private sector by importing skilled managers and other professionals. This need not mean a completely open-door policy where foreigners, unaware of our culture and traditions, take over top managerial posts. In the short run, there are more than enough skilled West Indians overseas who, under the right circumstances, would be willing to return to the region.

The productivity of labor in the Caribbean needs to be upgraded. This has to be tackled both within the individual enterprise and in the society as a whole. Firms need to put more emphasis on vocational and on-the-job training. For the society as a whole, education will have to become the first priority; that is, the financial requirements of what is needed for a well-educated work force should be the first priority on the budgets of regional governments.

Having a well-educated work force is not necessarily going to mean spending more money, but it will require that expenditures be allocated differently so that more can be achieved by the same amount of money. It will be necessary to reorder the educational curriculum at both the primary and secondary levels, putting more emphasis on mathematics and science. This can be achieved by increasing the number of classroom hours devoted to these subjects, accompanied by a corresponding reduction in other subjects. This kind of program for education would create a technologically oriented work force with a sound educational foundation, capable of high productivity, oriented to learning new technology, and adaptable to new job skills.

V. CONCLUSIONS

The process of integrating Caricom has involved small, externally vulnerable economies that are highly open, with extreme concentration of exports in primary products and a few markets. Despite aggregation into a collective involving liberalized trade, Caricom has not achieved a size sufficient to attain the economies of scale or prompt diversification of production and exports. Aggregation has not reduced the external vulnerability of these economies. The principal benefit has been in cooperating to negotiate or bargain as a group, which could have been undertaken without committing to economic integration.

Against the background of the limited achievements of Caricom, and indeed its declining significance to the trade of member countries, the question arises whether Caricom can further the economic diversification and development of member countries. Should there be a deepening or widening? Deepening will not enhance economic integration because it cannot overcome the limitations of inadequate critical mass in terms of market size. Therefore, widening seems to be the option Caricom should pursue. This choice is reinforced by developments and trends in the global economy, which indicate the emergence of large, regional trade blocs that dwarf Caricom.

Caricom must move with alacrity toward widening, given the imminence of NAFTA. However, what ultimately will determine the economic achievements of Caricom member states will be improved economic efficiency, export competitiveness, and economic diversification, which in turn will result from internal processes of reform and structural adjustment.

NOTES

1. Gordon K. Lewis, *The Growth of the Modern West Indies* (New York: Monthly Review Press, 1969), 343–67.

2. W. Andrew Axline, *Caribbean Integration: The Politics of Regionalism* (London: Frances Printer, 1979), 84–90.

3. Harold Brewster and Clive Y. Thomas, *The Dynamics of West Indian Economic Integration* (Mona, Jamaica: Institute of Social and Economic Research, University of the West Indies, 1967).

4. United Nations Economic Commission for Latin America and the Caribbean.

5. Trevor Harker, *Caribbean Integration in the Changing Global Context*, Economic Commission for Latin American and the Caribbean, WP/91/3 (October 31, 1991): 6.

6. Richard L. Bernal, "Caribbean Debt Relief," *Caribbean Affairs* 4, no. 2 (June 1991): 45–58.

7. *Caribbean Region Current Economic Situation, Regional Issues and Capital Inflows*, World Bank Report No. 8246-CRG (February 22, 1990): 8–9.

8. Ibid.

9. Richard L. Bernal, "Regional Trade Arrangements in the Western Hemisphere," *American University Journal of International Law and Policy* 8, no. 4 (summer 1993): 683–718.

10. *Potential Effects of a North American Free Trade Agreement on Apparel Investment in CBERA Countries*, United States International Trade Commission, Publication 2542 (July 1992): vii.

11. Richard L. Bernal, Statement before the House Ways and Means Subcommittee on Trade, North American Free Trade Agreement Hearing, September 22, 1992.

12. *Time for Action: The Report of the West Indian Commission* (Black Rock, Barbados: West Indian Commission, 1992), 445–46.

13. Fourth ACP-EEC Convention signed on December 15, 1989, *The Courier*, no. 120 (March-April 1990): 166.

14. Norman Girvan, "Reflections on Regional Integration and Disintegration," in *Integration and Participatory Development*, ed. Judith Wedderburn (Kingston: Friedrich Ebert Stiftung, 1990), 6.

15. Richard Crawford, *In the Era of Human Capital* (New York: Harper Collins, 1991).

16. Stan Davis and Bill Davidson, *2020 Vision* (New York: Simon and Schuster, 1991); Shoshana Zuboff, *In the Age of the Smart Machine* (New York: Basic Books, 1988).

17. Richard O'Brien, *Global Financial Integration: The End of Geography* (New York: Council on Foreign Relations Press, 1992).

18. Joseph L. Badaracco, Jr., *The Knowledge Link: How Firms Compete through Strategic Alliances* (Boston: Harvard Business School Press, 1991).

19. Yves Doz, "International Industries: Fragmentation Versus Globalization," in *Technology and Global Industry*, ed. Bruce R. Guile and Harry Brocks (Washington D.C.: National Academy Press, 1987), 115.

CONTRIBUTORS

Richard Bernal
Ambassador of Jamaica to the United States, Permanent Representative to the Organization of American States (OAS), and Chairman of the OAS Working Group on the Enterprise for the Americas Initiative

Roberto Bouzas
Professor of International Economics, Universidad de Buenos Aires, and Senior Fellow, International Relations Area, Facultad Latinoamericana de Cienias Sociales (FLACSO), Buenos Aires, Argentina

Andrea Butelmann
Senior Researcher, Corporación de Investigaciones Económicas para Latinoamerica (CIEPLAN), Santiago, Chile

Pilar Esguerra
Advisor to the Colombian Foreign Trade Board and Senior Researcher, Fundación para la Educación Superior y el Desarrollo (FEDESARROLLO), Bototá, Colombia

Winston Fritsch
Professor of Economics, Departmento de Economia, Pontificia Universidade Catolica do Rio de Janeiro, Rio de Janeiro, Brazil

Nora Lustig
Senior Fellow, Foreign Policy Studies, Brookings Institution, Washington, D.C., USA

José Antonio Ocampo
Minister of Agriculture, Colombia; former Director of the Fundación para la Educación Superior y el Desarrollo (FEDE-SARROLLO), Bogotá, Colombia

Ennio Rodríguez
Principal Strategic Planning Officer, Inter American Development Bank, Washington, D.C., USA

Jaime Ros
Professor of Economics and Fellow at the Helen Kellogg Institute for International Studies, University of Notre Dame, Notre Dame, USA

Alexandre A. Tombini
Professor of Economics, Departamento de Economia, Universidade de Brasília, Brasilia, Brazil